Editorials

ジャパンタイムズ
社説集

2020年

編▶ ジャパンタイムズ出版 英語出版編集部

下半期 | 7月▶12月

July to December 2020

the japan
times
出版

2020年下半期の世界と日本

7 月

● **香港国家安全維持法で初の逮捕者**

中国への抗議活動を規制する「香港国家安全維持法」が6月30日深夜に施行。翌日の返還記念日に大規模な抗議デモが行われ、逮捕者に初めて国安法が適用された。

● **レジ袋有料化がスタート**

全国でプラスチック製買物袋が有料に。小売業を営むすべての事業者に義務付け。

● **ロシア、全国投票で憲法改正が成立**

憲法改正の全国投票が行われ、賛成77.92%で成立が決定。プーチン大統領の長期続投が可能となる。

● **九州豪雨で大きな被害**

熊本県南部を中心に九州・中部地方で激しい雨が降り続き、甚大な被害に。

● **英も中国通信機器最大手のファーウェイ排除へ**

米国による規制強化に続き、英国が5G通信網からファーウェイ排除を発表。

● **小池氏が都知事続投**

東京都知事選挙で現職の小池百合子知事が全体の60%近くの票を獲得し、再選。

● **台湾、李登輝元総統が逝去**

「台湾民主化の父」と呼ばれた李登輝元総統が多臓器不全のため死去。

● **「Go To キャンペーン」開始**

コロナが収束しない中、旅行代金の一部をクーポンなどで還元する「Go To トラベル」がスタート。

8月

● 安倍首相が辞任を表明
持病の潰瘍性大腸炎が再発したことを理由に辞任を発表。第2次政権の在任日数は2,822日(7年8カ月超)。

● レバノンの首都ベイルートで爆発
ベイルートの港湾地区で大規模な爆発が連続して発生。倉庫に保管されていた大量の化学物質に引火したと見られ、多数の死傷者が出た。

● イスラエルとアラブ首長国連邦が国交正常化で合意
両国が国交正常化に合意したとトランプ米大統領が発表。イスラエルとアラブ諸国の国交正常化は26年ぶり。

● 広島・長崎が75回目の原爆忌
原爆投下から75年。広島と長崎では、コロナ禍で規模を縮小して平和記念式典が行われた。

● モーリシャス島沖の重油流出被害が深刻に
インド洋のモーリシャス沖で日本の貨物船が座礁し、重油が流出。サンゴ礁をはじめとする海洋生態系への深刻な影響が懸念される。

● 米西部カリフォルニア州の山火事で非常事態宣言
カリフォルニアで山火事が多発。オレゴン、ワシントンへと広がり、計2万平方キロメートル超が焼失、50万人超が避難対象に。

● シンガポール独立55周年
マレーシアから分離・独立して55年目の独立記念日を迎え、全国で記念行事が開催。

● ベラルーシ大統領選に不正疑惑
ルカシェンコ大統領の6選に不正得票の疑い。大規模な抗議デモが国内各地で多発した。

9月

●ルース・ギンズバーグ米連邦最高裁判事が逝去
膵臓がんによる合併症のため87歳で死去。女性の権利向上に尽力した。

●菅内閣が発足
衆参両議院が本会議で菅義偉自民党総裁を第99代総理大臣に指名。

●セルビアとコソボ、経済関係正常化で合意
旧ユーゴスラビアの両国首脳が米ホワイトハウスを訪れ、合意書に署名した。

●スーダン、ナイル川で洪水
アフリカのスーダンを流れるナイル川で洪水が発生。10万棟の家屋が全半壊、50万人に影響。

●大坂なおみ選手、2年ぶりに全米オープン制す
人種差別への抗議を示す姿勢が話題に。1回戦から決勝まで、黒人犠牲者の名前が記された7枚のマスクを着用した。

●アフガン停戦協議始まる
アフガニスタン政府と反政府武装勢力タリバン間で恒久停戦に向けた初の協議が開始。

●欧州連合、中国の少数民族政策に懸念表明
欧州連合(EU)首脳は中国の習近平国家主席とオンライン会議を行い、少数民族ウイグル族やチベット族への人権抑圧に懸念を表明した。

●サグラダ・ファミリア教会、2026年の完成は不可能
コロナ流行の影響で、ガウディ没後100年に当たる2026年の完成はほぼ不可能になったと建設責任者がコメント。

●アルメニアに戒厳令
アルメニアとアゼルバイジャンの係争地をめぐり、両軍が衝突。

10月

● **トランプ米大統領夫妻がコロナ感染**

大統領が自身のツイッターアカウントで、ウイルス検査で陽性と投稿。

● **核兵器禁止条約、発効へ**

条約の批准国と地域が、発効に必要な50に達した。批准手続き終了から90日後の2021年1月に発効となる。

● **東西ドイツ統一から30年**

各地で30周年を祝う一方で、世論調査によると半数の国民が今なお経済格差など社会の溝を感じているという。

● **世界食糧計画（WFP）がノーベル平和賞**

授賞理由は、飢餓との闘いや、飢えを紛争の武器として利用することを防ぐ取り組み。

● **邦人男性がマチュピチュを「独占」**

コロナによる遺跡閉鎖と移動制限のため、麓の村で200日以上を過ごした邦人男性が、ペルー政府の計らいで唯一の観光客として遺跡を訪問。

● **ニュージーランド総選挙、与党労働党が圧勝**

コロナ対策で手腕を発揮したアーダーン首相率いる労働党が、過半数の64議席を獲得。

● **ローマ教皇、同性婚に一定の理解**

ドキュメンタリー映画で同性カップルを法的に保護する「シビルユニオン」支持の立場を示した。

● **チリ国民投票、新憲法制定を支持**

独裁政権時代に制定された現行憲法に代わる新憲法制定が決定。

11月

● ジョー・バイデン米大統領誕生へ
大接戦となった米大統領選は、バイデン氏が過半数獲得を確実にし、副大統領となる
カマラ・ハリス氏と勝利宣言を行った。

● 大阪の都構想、住民投票は反対多数
住民投票の結果は僅差で反対が賛成を上回り、大阪市は存続へ。

● 秋篠宮さま「立皇嗣の礼」
天皇陛下の弟、秋篠宮さまが皇位継承順位第1位となったことを国内外に宣言。

● ミャンマー総選挙、与党が単独過半数を確保
アウン・サン・スー・チー氏率いる与党の国民民主連盟(NLD)が圧勝。スー・チー政権の
継続が確定した。

● リオのカーニバル、7月に延期
コロナ感染拡大の影響により、パレード主催団体が7月に延期することを発表。

● ソフトバンク、4年連続日本一
福岡ソフトバンクホークスが読売ジャイアンツとの日本シリーズを4連勝で制し、4年連続
日本一に輝いた。

● NYのクオモ州知事に国際エミー賞
国際テレビ芸術科学アカデミーが国際エミー賞の功労賞をクオモ州知事に授与すると発
表。感染拡大が続くニューヨークで100日以上毎日、会見を行った。

12月

●**映画『劇場版「鬼滅の刃」無限列車編』が歴代1位**

28日に興行収入324億円を記録し、『千と千尋の神隠し』(316.8億円)を抜いて歴代興行収入ランキング1位に。

●**小惑星探査機「はやぶさ2」カプセル帰還**

カプセルには小惑星「リュウグウ」のものと見られる砂の粒が確認された。

●**イラン、核開発拡大法が成立**

イラン護憲評議会が核開発の大幅な拡大を政府に義務付ける法案を承認。

●**新型コロナウイルスのワクチン接種開始**

米国や欧州など世界各地で、米ファイザー社、モデルナ社のワクチン接種が本格化。

●**英で変異ウイルス拡大**

ジョンソン英首相が、感染力が高い新型コロナウイルスの変異種が広がっていると発表。その後、日本を含む各地で感染者が確認された。

●**デモが続くタイで地方選**

反体制デモが続くタイで76県の首長と議員を選ぶ地方選が実施。野党系の首長選出はならず。

●**大雪により関越自動車道で車両取り残され**

新潟県、群馬県などの大雪により、関越自動車道で計2,000台以上が立ち往生。解消まで2日を要した。

目次

エディター／霜村 和久
編集協力／堀内 友子
カバーデザイン／日下 充典
本文デザイン／ハーモナイズデザイン（松森 雅孝、柳沢 由美子）
写真提供／共同通信社
ナレーター／クリス・コブロウスキー、ハンナ・グレース

●音声収録時間／約86分

新型コロナウイルスが与えた影響

その他の社会問題

● 監修・執筆者紹介

又江原 裕 （またえばら・ゆたか）

1935年生まれ。早稲田大学政治経済学部卒業。
ジャパンタイムズ論説顧問。
同社編集局長、主幹、専務などを歴任後、現職。

● 翻訳・語注執筆者紹介（50音順）

宇都宮 まどか （うつのみや・まどか）

1968年生まれ。州立カリフォルニア大学バークレー校政治学科卒業。ジャパンタイムズ
「週刊ST」、「Japan Times Weekly」主任を経て、翻訳者、英語学習アドバイザー。
訳書に『英語で読むからよくわかる チューデイ先生のなるほど英語レッスン超基本編』
（ジャパンタイムズ出版）。

桑田 健 （くわた・たけし）

1965年生まれ。東京外国語大学英米語学科卒業。
訳書に『痛いほど君が好きなのに』（ヴィレッジブックス）、『マギの聖骨』『AIの魔女』などの
「シグマフォース・シリーズ」、「THE HUNTERSシリーズ」、「タッカー＆ケイン・シリーズ」
（以上、竹書房）、『地球 驚異の自然現象』（河出書房）、『ビッグデータベースボール』『ア
ストロボール』『プロジェクト・ネメシス』『プロジェクト・マイゴ』（以上、KADOKAWA）、
『セックス・イン・ザ・シー』（講談社）などがある。

小川 貴宏 （こかわ・たかひろ）

1962年生まれ。東京外国語大学英米語学科卒業。
同大学修士課程（ゲルマン系言語専攻）修了。英国 Exeter University で応用言語学修士
号を取得。防衛大学校准教授を経て、現在、成蹊大学教授。
著書に『Sound Right! 14のグループで覚える英語の発音』、翻訳・解説執筆に『英語で見
る！聴く！BBCドキュメンタリー＆ドラマ BOOK 1』（以上、ジャパンタイムズ出版）がある。

中村 直子 （なかむら・なおこ）

1951年生まれ。上智大学英米文学科卒業。
元ジャパンタイムズ「週刊ST」副編集長。
翻訳・解説執筆に『英語で読む旧約聖書』『英語で読む新約聖書』、編著書に『身の回りのこ
とが何でも言える 英会話ぷち表現』、訳書に『英語で読む源氏物語（上）（下）』『英語で読
む平家物語（上）（下）』『英語で読む古典落語』『英語で読む世界昔話 Book 1 ～5』（以上、
ジャパンタイムズ出版）などがある。

MP3音声のご利用案内

本書に掲載されているすべての英文記事の読上げ音声を、無料でダウンロードし、お聞きいただくことができます。

※「2020年上半期」版より、付属CDのご提供を終了いたしました。

スマートフォン 📱

1. ジャパンタイムズ出版の音声アプリ「OTO Navi」をインストール

2. OTO Naviで本書を検索
3. OTO Naviで音声をダウンロードし、再生

3秒早送り・早戻し、繰り返し再生などの便利機能つき。学習にお役立てください。

パソコン 💻

1. ブラウザからジャパンタイムズ出版のサイト「BOOK CLUB」にアクセス

https://bookclub.japantimes.co.jp/book/b556375.html

2. 「ダウンロード」ボタンをクリック
3. 音声をダウンロードし、iTunesなどに取り込んで再生

※音声はzipファイルを展開(解凍)してご利用ください。

第1章 国際

11月24日、地元デラウェア州ウィルミントンで演説をするバイデン次期米国大統領

Dangerous tensions at the top of the world—again

世界のてっぺんでの危険な緊張が再燃

September 3, 2020 　　　　　　　　●Tracks 02-08 / 訳 pp. 42-44

Track 02

1　Tensions between India and China are rising again. This summer, the two countries' militaries clashed in Ladakh along the Line of Actual Control, their contested border in the Himalaya region. The loss of more than 30 lives sobered both governments, prompting military talks that made little progress. Late last month, there was another confrontation between the two armies— fortunately verbal, not physical—that underscored the fragility of the cease-fire.

2　Hostility is infecting the broader relationship. The general public in both countries are increasingly antagonistic to the other and the Delhi government has launched an economic offensive against its northern neighbor. Since both nations are headed by nationalists, the prospect of more clashes and escalation is real.

Track 03

3　India and China have long contested their 3,500-km border, the Line of Actual Control. They fought a war in 1962 (which India lost) and have clashed several times since. The possibility of escalation prompted them to adopt rules of engagement in 1993 in which both sides banned border patrols from using firearms.

4　That worked until last June, when each country accused the other of encroachment. Hundreds of troops were deployed from each side, and one evening in mid-June they brawled. It was no less deadly for the absence of firearms: Soldiers used rocks, sticks,

近年のインドと中国の国境問題は比較的平穏だったが、6月に衝突が発生し、死者も出た。両国が互いに相手を非難し、国民感情も悪化。新型コロナウイルス感染症の流行もあって、早期の解決が見えない状態だ。これ以上の拡大に発展しないことを願う。

1
- □ [タイトル]tension 緊張
- □ clash 衝突する
- □ Line of Actual Control 実効支配線
  →インドと中国の国境紛争地帯の境界線
- □ contested 争われた、係争中の
- □ border 国境
- □ region 地方、地域
- □ sober 目を覚まさせる
- □ prompt 促す

- □ military talks 軍事交渉
- □ progress 進展
- □ confrontation 対立、衝突
- □ verbal 言葉による
- □ physical 身体的な
- □ underscore 強調する
- □ fragility もろさ
- □ cease-fire 停戦

2
- □ hostility 敵意
- □ infect 伝染する、波及する
- □ increasingly ますます
- □ antagonistic 敵対心のある
- □ the Delhi government インド政府
- □ launch 開始する

- □ economic offensive 経済攻勢
- □ northern neighbor 北の隣国→ここでは中国のこと
- □ nationalist 国家主義者
- □ prospect 可能性、見通し
- □ escalation 事態の拡大

3
- □ contest 争う
- □ possibility 可能性
- □ adopt 採用する
- □ rules of engagement 交戦規定→軍隊がどんな場面でどんな武器を使用するか定めたもの

- □ ban 禁止する
- □ border patrol 国境警備隊
- □ firearm(s) 火器

4
- □ accuse A of B AをBだと非難する
- □ encroachment 領土侵犯
- □ troop 部隊、兵士
- □ deploy 配備する
- □ mid-June 6月半ば

- □ brawl けんかする
- □ no less 同様に
- □ deadly 致命的な
- □ absence 欠如、ないこと

clubs and bare fists, and for the first time since the 1970s, lives were lost. Several dozen troops were killed—the Chinese never admitted their casualties—and a dozen or so Indian troops taken hostage (and eventually released).

Track 04

5 The wounds have festered since, especially among Indians. The Indian Army said it would no longer abide by the old rules of engagement. In early July, Indian Prime Minister Narendra Modi, along with other senior officials, visited Ladakh, offering support for the troops and promises of infrastructure spending, both of which signaled to Beijing his concern about the issue.

6 Several rounds of negotiations followed and just two weeks ago, the two governments agreed to resolve problems in an "expeditious manner" and in accordance with existing protocols. India's Foreign Ministry released a statement that affirmed that "The two sides will continue to sincerely work toward complete disengagement of the troops along the Line of Actual Control."

Track 05

7 That report was followed days later by news that both sides had sent more troops to the area and were digging in. India accused China of building observation towers, bunkers and marinas in disputed territory, and said that these moves "violated the previous consensus" and constituted "provocative military movements." Troops from both sides were said to have come within a meter of each other and engaged in yelling matches before being separated. A Tibetan member of an Indian special forces unit died in a mine blast near the site of a flare-up with Chinese troops.

□ bare fist 素手
□ dozen 1ダースの、10余りの
　→ several dozen は「数十の」の意
□ casualty 死傷者

□ ... or so …ほど
□ (be) taken hostage 人質に取られる
□ eventually のちに、最終的に
□ release 解放する

5
□ fester （傷が）膿む
□ abide by ... …に従う
□ prime minister 首相
□ along with ... …とともに
□ senior official 高官

□ infrastructure インフラ
□ spending 支出
□ signal 合図を送る
□ concern 懸念

6
□ round （会議などの）1回、ラウンド
□ negotiation 交渉
□ resolve 解決する
□ expeditious 迅速な
□ in accordance with ... …に従って
□ existing 既存の
□ protocol 協定

□ foreign ministry 外務省
□ statement 声明
□ affirm 確約する
□ sincerely 真摯に
□ complete 完全な
□ disengagement 撤退

7
□ dig in （塹壕を掘って）守りを固める
□ observation tower 監視塔
□ bunker 掩蔽壕（えんぺいごう）
□ marina 係留地点
□ disputed territory 紛争地域
□ violate 違反する
□ previous 以前の
□ consensus 合意
□ constitute …に等しい

□ provocative 挑発的な
□ engage in ... …に関わる
□ yelling match 怒鳴り合い
□ separate 引き離す
□ special forces unit 特殊部隊
□ mine 地雷
□ blast 爆発
□ flare-up 再発

8   According to a spokesperson for China's Foreign Ministry, Chinese troops "never cross the Line of Actual Control." A spokesperson for the People's Liberation Army denounced the Indian Army for a "flagrant provocation" by crossing the Line of Actual Control. Rhetorical retrenchment narrows the space for the "mutually agreed reciprocal actions" that India insists upon.

Track 06

9   A growing troop presence makes real the prospect of another armed clash. That inclination is reinforced by a perception that Mr. Modi mishandled the June incident, when he initially played down its severity. Indian officials, and especially those in the military, are disenchanted with mechanisms to deal with the military standoff, arguing that China is changing the status quo.

10   Chinese strategists counter that India is the revisionist, pointing to Delhi's decision last year to change the status of the state of Jammu and Kashmir, territory held by India but claimed by Pakistan, separate Ladakh from it, and to administer the region as a union territory. For them, that demanded a Chinese response.

Track 07

11   India is advancing on a second front, adopting measures that restrict Chinese access to the Indian economy. Even before the first clash, India had changed rules to require government approval of all investment from China. It has further tightened investment restrictions, imposed tariffs on a wide range of imports from China, banned nearly 180 Chinese apps and told local telecommunications companies to phase out equipment from Chinese companies like Huawei and ZTE.

8
- according to ... …によると
- spokesperson 報道官
- the People's Liberation Army 人民解放軍
- denounce 非難する
- flagrant あからさまな
- provocation 挑発行為
- rhetorical retrenchment 言葉を並べるばかりの自己防衛→rhetorical は「修辞的な」、retrenchment は「守りを固めること」
- mutually 相互に
- reciprocal action 相互作用
- insist 強く主張する

9
- presence 駐留
- make real ... …を現実的にする
- armed clash 武力衝突
- inclination 傾向
- reinforce 強化する
- perception 認識
- mishandle 処理を誤る
- incident 事件
- play down ... …を軽視する
- severity 深刻さ
- be disenchanted with ... …に幻滅する
- mechanism 仕組み、手順
- standoff 膠着状態
- the status quo 現状

10
- strategist 戦略家
- counter 反論する
- revisionist 修正主義者
- point to ... …を指摘する
- territory 領土
- claim （所有権を）主張する
- administer 統治する
- union territory 連邦直轄領
- demand 必要とする
- response 反応、対応

11
- advance 進む
- front 戦線
- restrict 制限する
- require 必要とする
- approval 認可
- investment 投資
- tighten 厳しくする
- restriction 制限
- impose tariffs on ... …に関税を課す
- a wide range of ... 広範囲に及ぶ…
- app アプリ→application (software) の略
- telecommunication(s) 電気通信
- phase out ... …を段階的に廃止する
- equipment 機器

12 While restrictions will hurt both sides—China's share of India's total imports more than quadrupled, increasing from less than 3 percent in 2000 to 14 percent in 2018—Indian sentiment has hardened with many consumers backing a "boycott China" movement. Anger is rising in China as well. According to an August Global Times poll, more than 70 percent of Chinese believed that India was too hostile to them and nearly 90 percent supported their government's "retaliation against Indian provocations."

`Track 08`

13 Nationalist leaders, the general antagonistic public, military confrontations and nuclear-armed neighbors: This is as dangerous a combination as can be imagined. Diplomacy and top-level intervention are ever more urgent, yet ever more difficult in a pandemic. A face-saving formula for mutual redeployments and a retreat by both militaries are essential first steps.

12
- □ share 割合、シェア
- □ quadruple 4倍になる
- □ sentiment 感情
- □ harden 硬化する
- □ consumer 消費者
- □ back 支持する
- □ boycott ボイコットする
- □ Global Times 環球時報→中国共産党系の新聞
- □ poll 世論調査
- □ hostile 敵対的な
- □ retaliation 報復

13
- □ nuclear-armed 核武装した
- □ combination 組み合わせ
- □ diplomacy 外交
- □ top-level 首脳レベルの
- □ intervention 調停、仲介
- □ urgent 急を要する
- □ pandemic パンデミック、(疫病の)世界的大流行
- □ face-saving メンツを保つ
- □ formula 解決策
- □ mutual 相互の
- □ redeployment 配置転換、移動
- □ retreat 撤退
- □ essential 必要不可欠な

Apparent poisoning of Alexei Navalny reveals Mr. Putin's world

毒殺未遂疑惑があらわにしたプーチン大統領の世界

September 10, 2020　　　　　●Tracks 09-14 / 訳 pp. 45-47

Track 09

1　The list of outrages committed by the government of Russian President Vladimir Putin is long and growing. The most recent is the alleged poison attack on opposition leader Alexei Navalny, who fell ill while on a plane in Russia last month. Mr. Navalny was evacuated to Germany for treatment, where tests revealed that he had been poisoned with a nerve agent. The Russian government denies the charge but evidence and logic support the accusation. Now, the world must do more than serve up pro forma verbal condemnations of this barbarism; diplomacy as usual will only encourage more of such actions.

2　Mr. Navalny is the highest-profile opposition leader in Russia. For over a decade, he has denounced the government and ruling parties for systematic corruption in a campaign that has taken root across the country. He has been jailed 13 times, and given a six-year prison sentence for embezzlement. Mr. Navalny insists those charges were a pretext to silence him: The conviction bans him from running against Mr. Putin in elections.

Track 10

3　Apparently, preventing him from running was not enough. Instead, Mr. Navalny had to be silenced. On a flight from Siberia to Moscow, Mr. Navalny fell violently ill, forcing the plane to divert to the city of Omsk. He was admitted to a hospital there. Russian officials refused to allow him to be evacuated to Germany for treatment

▼ About This Editorial ▼

ロシアの反体制派指導者アレクセイ・ナワリヌイ氏が８月20日、毒物で襲撃されたと見られる事件が発生。G7外相は９月９日、ロシア政府を非難する共同声明を出して真相究明を求めたが、度重なるロシアの蛮行に対して国際社会はより厳しい措置を取るべきだ。

1
- □ [タイトル]apparent …らしい
- □ [タイトル]poisoning 毒を盛ること
- □ [タイトル]reveal 明らかにする
- □ outrage 非道な行為
- □ commit 犯す
- □ alleged 疑われている
- □ opposition leader 野党党首、反体制派指導者
- □ fall ill 具合が悪くなる
- □ be evacuated 搬送される
- □ treatment 治療
- □ nerve agent 神経ガス
- □ deny 否定する
- □ charge 疑惑、嫌疑
- □ evidence 証拠
- □ logic 論理
- □ accusation 非難、告発
- □ serve up 再々持ち出す
- □ pro forma 形式上の
- □ verbal 言葉の
- □ condemnation 非難、糾弾
- □ barbarism 野蛮な行為
- □ diplomacy 外交
- □ ... as usual 従来通りの…

2
- □ highest-profile 最も注目を浴びる
- □ decade 10年
- □ denounce 糾弾する
- □ ruling party 与党
- □ systematic 組織的な
- □ corruption 汚職
- □ take root 根付く
- □ be jailed 投獄される
- □ prison sentence 実刑判決
- □ embezzlement 横領
- □ insist 主張する
- □ pretext 口実
- □ silence 沈黙させる
- □ conviction 有罪判決
- □ ban ... from *doing* …に対し~することを禁じる
- □ run against ... …の対立候補として立候補する

3
- □ apparently どうやら…のようだ
- □ prevent ... from *doing* …が~するのを妨げる
- □ violently ひどく
- □ force ... to *do* …に~することを余儀なくさせる
- □ divert 方向転換する
- □ Omsk オムスク→ロシア中南部の都市
- □ be admitted to a hospital 入院する
- □ official 当局者
- □ refuse to *do* ~することを拒む
- □ allow 許可する

despite the urgings of his wife and supporters. Three days later, that decision was reversed and he was allowed to go to Berlin.

4   German doctors and chemical weapons experts say their tests provide "unequivocal proof" that Mr. Navalny was poisoned with a Soviet-era nerve agent, novichok. Russia denies the allegation, noting that the Russian doctors in Omsk found no evidence of poison and has demanded that the German government share the test results.

Track 11

5   Berlin should oblige, but it will make no difference to Moscow. The Russian government has made no secret of its readiness to silence opposition by any means, anywhere. There have been at least six attempts to poison dissidents in the past five years, some in Russia, some in other countries. Mr. Navalny says that he was poisoned during one of his stays in jail. This time, it is believed that he was dosed by tea he drank in the airport before boarding the plane.

6   Novichok is a powerful nerve agent that was developed and weaponized by the Soviet Union during the Cold War. Its existence was revealed by a Russian defector; Moscow never declared it when Russian chemical weapon stockpiles were destroyed pursuant to the Chemical Weapons Convention. No other country is known to have developed novichok and the sophistication of the production process means that only governments would have it.

□ despite …にもかかわらず
□ urging 懇願
□ supporter 支持者

□ decision 決定
□ be reversed 覆される

4
□ chemical weapon(s) 化学兵器
□ expert 専門家
□ provide 示す、提供する
□ unequivocal 疑う余地のない
□ proof 証拠
□ Soviet-era ソビエト連邦時代の
□ novichok ノビチョク→旧ソ連が軍用に

開発した化学兵器で、ロシア語で「新参者」の意
□ allegation 主張、申し立て
□ note 指摘する
□ evidence 形跡
□ demand 要求する
□ test result 検査結果

5
□ Berlin ドイツ政府
□ oblige 応じる
□ make no difference to ... …にとってはどちらでもよい
□ Moscow ロシア政府
□ make no secret of ... …を隠さない
□ readiness 準備ができていること
□ by any means あらゆる手段を使って

□ anywhere どこでも
□ at least 少なくとも
□ attempt 試み
□ dissident 反体制派
□ past 過去の
□ jail 刑務所
□ dose （薬を）与える
□ board 搭乗する

6
□ be developed 開発される
□ be weaponized 兵器化される
□ the Soviet Union ソビエト連邦
□ the Cold War 冷戦
□ existence 存在
□ defector 亡命者→米国に亡命した化学者でノビチョク開発者のビル・ミルザヤノフ氏のこと
□ declare 申告する

□ stockpile 備蓄品
□ be destroyed 廃棄される
□ pursuant to ... …に基づいて
□ Chemical Weapons Convention 化学兵器禁止条約
□ be known to have *done* ～したことで知られる
□ sophistication 複雑さ
□ production process 生産工程

Track 12

7 Equally damning, novichok was used to attack former Russian spy Sergei Skripal and his daughter in England in 2018. Six people were poisoned in that incident; one person—not Mr. Skripal—died after picking up the perfume bottle that had been used to transport the poison and was carelessly thrown away after its use. Novichok's provenance, its use against perceived enemies of the Kremlin and Moscow's insouciance when it comes to such charges all support Russian government involvement.

8 It is that last point that is most damning and which demands action. The Kremlin is well served by a belief that there is no line it will not cross to silence its enemies and that it cannot be stopped. There is no other explanation for the use of polonium to murder former spy and Russian government critic Alexander Litvinenko in 2006. Radiation from the poison left an easily followed trail that showed where the killers stayed, where they ate, the planes on which they traveled to and from Russia and even the seats they occupied during flights.

Track 13

9 Individual governments and the European Union have demanded an investigation by Moscow into the Navalny case but that is not enough. The G7 took a first step this week when its foreign ministers "condemned in the strongest possible terms the confirmed poisoning" of Mr. Navalny, but the pledge to "monitor closely" Russia's response to calls for an explanation of "the hideous poisoning" sounds weak.

7
- □ equally 同様に
- □ damning 罪を明らかにする
- □ former 元…
- □ incident 事件
- □ pick up 拾う
- □ perfume 香水
- □ transport 運ぶ
- □ be thrown away 捨てられる
- □ carelessly 不用意に
- □ provenance 出所
- □ perceived …と見なされている
- □ enemy 敵
- □ Kremlin ロシア政府
- □ insouciance 無頓着さ
- □ when it comes to ... …のこととなると
- □ involvement 関与

8
- □ be well served by a belief that ... …であると心得ている
- □ cross 越える
- □ there is no other ... ほかに…がない
- □ polonium ポロニウム→猛毒の放射性物質
- □ murder 殺害する
- □ critic 批判者
- □ Alexander Litvinenko アレクサンドル・リトビネンコ氏→元ロシア連邦保安庁中佐でのちに英国に亡命し、ロシアに対する反体制活動家となった
- □ radiation 放射線
- □ leave 残す
- □ trail 痕跡
- □ killer 殺害者
- □ to and from 往復
- □ occupy (席などを)とる

9
- □ individual governments 各国政府
- □ the European Union 欧州連合
- □ investigation 調査
- □ case 事件
- □ G7 主要7カ国
- □ foreign minister 外務大臣
- □ condemn 非難する
- □ term 表現
- □ confirmed 確認された
- □ pledge 誓約
- □ monitor closely 注視する
- □ response 反応
- □ call 呼び掛け
- □ hideous 恐ろしい
- □ sound …のように聞こえる、思われる

10   Russia must be punished for its murderous actions and Mr. Putin stripped of the delusion that he is untouchable. There cannot be business as usual. Europe should reassess its position on the Nord Stream 2 gas pipeline, which will supply gas from Russia. Once sacrosanct, Germany's foreign minister has suggested that it may now be on the table. German Chancellor Angela Merkel has indicated that she agrees. In a sign of Paris's anger, France has postponed a long-sought visit to Moscow by the country's foreign and defense ministers.

`Track 14`

11   There is a temptation to believe that since this act occurred on Russian soil, other countries' options are limited. That is wrong. There is no evidence to suggest that Russia believes that borders matter; it has acted as it sees fit, law be damned, wherever it wishes. It is a sobering reminder to Japan, and all governments, when they contemplate deals with Russia and Mr. Putin.

10
- □ be punished 罰せられる
- □ murderous 殺人の
- □ be stripped of ... …を剥ぎ取られる
- □ delusion 思い込み
- □ untouchable 無敵の
- □ business as usual いつも通りのこと
- □ reassess 見直す
- □ position 見解
- □ Nord Stream 2 gas pipeline 天然ガスのパイプライン、ノルドストリーム2→ロシア沿岸部とドイツを結ぶ
- □ supply 供給する
- □ sacrosanct 極めて神聖な、干渉を許さない
- □ suggest 示唆する
- □ be on the table 検討される
- □ German Chancellor ドイツ首相
- □ indicate 表明する
- □ a sign of ... …の表れ
- □ postpone 延期する
- □ long-sought 念願の
- □ defense minister 国防大臣

11
- □ temptation 誘惑
- □ act 行為
- □ occur 起こる
- □ soil 国土
- □ option 選択肢
- □ be limited 限られている
- □ border 国境
- □ matter 重要である
- □ as one sees fit 好きなように
- □ ... be damned …にはお構いなしだ
- □ sobering 身の引き締まるような、厳しい
- □ reminder 注意喚起
- □ contemplate もくろむ、期待する
- □ deal 交渉

U.N. fails to shine at its diamond jubilee

ダイヤモンド・ジュビリーを迎えても輝けない国連

September 24, 2020   ●Tracks 15-19 / 訳 pp. 48-49

Track 15

1　A diamond jubilee deserves more than prerecorded speeches, but somehow a parade of three-minute videos broadcast to a mostly empty General Assembly chamber succinctly captures the moment for the United Nations. The world is facing a set of crises that is unprecedented in modern history—the COVID-19 pandemic, a global economy that has gone off the rails and a climate catastrophe—and the world body is distracted by geopolitical rivalries and a growing tendency of national governments to go it alone while complaining about the institution's ineffectiveness. As U.N. Secretary General Antonio Guterres explained in comments at the world body's 75th anniversary, "we have a surplus of multilateral challenges and a deficit of multilateral solutions."

2　This is, warned Mr. Guterres, "a 1945 moment." The COVID pandemic has "laid bare the world's fragilities. … Climate calamity looms, biodiversity is collapsing, poverty is rising, hatred is spreading, geopolitical tensions are escalating, nuclear weapons remain on hair-trigger alert." Yet even in this precarious situation, cooperative action remains beyond reach.

▼ About This Editorial ▼

2020年に創設75周年を迎えた国連の総会では、新型コロナウイルス対策のため、事前録画の
ビデオによる各国首脳の演説が放映された。コロナ、世界経済、気候など世界は大問題を抱え
ているが、国連は機能不全に陥っている。その一因は、実状に合わなくなっている安全保障理
事会にある。

1
- □ [タイトル]diamond jubilee ダイヤモンド・ジュビリー、75年祭
- □ deserve 値する
- □ prerecord 事前に録音する
- □ a parade of ... …の行列
- □ General Assembly chamber 総会議場
- □ succinctly 端的に、簡潔に
- □ capture とらえる
- □ unprecedented 先例のない
- □ COVID-19 新型コロナウイルス感染症
- □ pandemic（疫病の）世界的大流行
- □ go off the rails 脱線する
- □ catastrophe 大変動、大災害
- □ the world body 世界的な団体→国連のこと。body は「団体、組織体」
- □ be distracted by ... …に悩まされる
- □ geopolitical 地政学的な
- □ rivalry 敵対行為、対抗意識
- □ go it alone 独力で物事を行う
- □ institution 機関→ここでは国連のこと
- □ ineffectiveness 無能さ、非効率性
- □ Secretary General 事務総長
- □ 75th anniversary 75周年記念
- □ surplus 剰余
- □ multilateral 多国間の
- □ challenge 問題
- □ deficit 不足

2
- □ "a 1945 moment"「1945年と同様の体験、1945年の追体験」
- □ lay bare さらけ出す
- □ fragility 脆弱さ、もろさ
- □ calamity 災害、惨事
- □ loom 迫る
- □ biodiversity 生物多様性
- □ collapse 崩壊する
- □ poverty 貧困
- □ spread 広がる
- □ tension 緊張
- □ escalate 増大する
- □ nuclear weapon 核兵器
- □ hair-trigger alert ヘアトリガー・アラート→米軍の核兵器を常時、即刻発射できる態勢を指す
- □ precarious 危うい
- □ situation 状況
- □ cooperative action 協調的な行動
- □ beyond reach 手が届かない

Track 16

3 There is plenty of blame to go around. The U.S. essentially snubbed the world body. Although U.S. President Donald Trump was listed first among the 182 heads of state or government to address Monday's commemoration, he did not deign to speak and instead dispatched the acting U.S. deputy U.N. ambassador who complained that for too long, the United Nations has resisted "meaningful reform," lacked transparency and was "too vulnerable to the agenda of autocratic regimes and dictatorships."

4 When he did speak to the body, in a short prerecorded address to the U.N. General Assembly later in the week, Mr. Trump was combative. He attacked China for unleashing the "China virus … this plague" upon the world. He denounced the Paris climate accord and the Iran nuclear deal and, as he did last year, urged other nations to emulate his "America First" policies.

Track 17

5 Other leaders, like Chinese President Xi Jinping and Russian President Vladimir Putin, urged countries to reject that view and embrace multilateralism and cooperation, but it is important to match words with deeds. They enjoy contrasting themselves with Mr. Trump—an easy way to look good—but they have been as obstinate in the protection of national prerogatives, as obstructionist in addressing problems and are no more eager to reform the U.N.—and in some cases have been even more reluctant than the U.S. to do so.

3
- ☐ blame 非難
- ☐ go around 行き渡る
- ☐ essentially 本質的に
- ☐ snub 肘鉄砲を食らわす、無視する
- ☐ address 演説する、式辞を述べる
- ☐ commemoration 記念式
- ☐ deign to *do* (もったいなくも)～して くださる→皮肉
- ☐ dispatch 派遣する、よこす
- ☐ acting 代理の
- ☐ deputy ambassador 次席大使
- ☐ resist 抵抗する
- ☐ meaningful 重要な、意味ある
- ☐ reform 改革
- ☐ transparency 透明性
- ☐ vulnerable 弱い、負けやすい
- ☐ agenda 政策
- ☐ autocratic regime 独裁政権
- ☐ dictatorship 独裁国家

4
- ☐ combative 戦闘的な
- ☐ attack 攻撃する
- ☐ unleash 解き放つ
- ☐ plague 伝染病、疫病
- ☐ denounce 非難する、糾弾する
- ☐ accord 協定
- ☐ nuclear deal 核合意
- ☐ urge ... to *do* …に～するよう勧める
- ☐ emulate 手本とする、見習う
- ☐ "America First"「米国第一」
- ☐ policy 政策

5
- ☐ reject 拒否する
- ☐ view 見方、考え方
- ☐ embrace (主義・思想などを)受け入れる
- ☐ multilateralism 多国間主義
- ☐ cooperation 協力、協調
- ☐ match words with deeds 言葉と行 為を一致させる
- ☐ contrast 対比させる、対照させて引き 立たせる
- ☐ obstinate 頑固に固執する、意固地な、 譲らない
- ☐ protection 保護
- ☐ prerogative 特権
- ☐ obstructionist 妨害者
- ☐ reluctant 気乗りしない、気の進まない

6   The focus of reform efforts is the Security Council, where five countries—China, France, Russia, the United States and the United Kingdom—have permanent seats and vetoes over its deliberations. Those seats reflected those countries' status as victors in World War II, but the world has been transformed in the 75 years since then and their power and privilege no longer reflect international reality. Nevertheless, those governments refuse to modernize the institution if it means that they will lose power. Equally important to them is the prospect of elevating rivals. Beijing has no desire to put either Japan or India, each a competitor for regional leadership, on the Security Council; Moscow is troubled by the idea of giving Germany that status or power. Their veto means that reform will not proceed. (Smaller regional rivals—Pakistan in the case of India, and Italy in the case of Germany—also oppose reform.)

`Track 18`

7   Japan remains committed to the vision of the United Nations articulated at its founding—a world united in a shared purpose: preventing war, promoting rule of law and the peaceful resolution of disputes, and ensuring human rights and equal opportunities for all peoples to be prosperous, healthy and participate in global governance. Even as successive Japanese governments have pushed to increase their defense capabilities, they have remained committed to diplomacy and multilateralism, and working through international institutions to address global challenges. Japan's push to reform the world body reflects a desire to do more, as the world's third leading economy should. In remarks at the commemoration, Foreign Minister Toshimitsu Motegi called for U.N. Security Council reform to make it "an effective and representative organ" of the 21st-century world. He reaffirmed Japan's readiness to take up the responsibilities of a permanent member of the U.N. Security Council, "and contribute to ensuring peace and stability of the world."

6
- ☐ focus 焦点
- ☐ effort(s) 取り組み
- ☐ the Security Council（国連の）安全保障理事会→米国・ロシア連邦・フランス・英国・中国の5常任理事国と非常任理事国10カ国から成る
- ☐ permanent seat 常任理事席
- ☐ veto 拒否権
- ☐ deliberation 審議
- ☐ reflect 反映する
- ☐ status 地位
- ☐ victor 戦勝国
- ☐ World War II 第二次世界大戦
- ☐ transform 変化する、変容する
- ☐ privilege 特権
- ☐ no longer もはや…ない
- ☐ reality 現実、実状
- ☐ nevertheless にもかかわらず
- ☐ refuse 拒否する
- ☐ modernize 近代化する、現代化する
- ☐ equally 同様に
- ☐ prospect 見通し
- ☐ elevate（地位、権力などを）高める
- ☐ rival 競争相手
- ☐ Beijing 中国政府
- ☐ desire 願望
- ☐ competitor 競争相手
- ☐ regional 地域の
- ☐ leadership 指導者の地位
- ☐ Moscow ロシア政府
- ☐ proceed 進む、前進する
- ☐ in the case of ... …の場合
- ☐ oppose 反対する

7
- ☐ commit 積極的に関わる
- ☐ vision 展望、ビジョン
- ☐ articulate 明示する
- ☐ founding 創設
- ☐ shared purpose 共通の目的
- ☐ prevent 防止する、予防する
- ☐ promote 促進する
- ☐ rule of law 法の支配
- ☐ resolution 解決
- ☐ dispute 紛争
- ☐ ensure 保証する
- ☐ human right 人権
- ☐ equal opportunity 機会均等
- ☐ prosperous 繁栄する
- ☐ participate in ... …に参加する
- ☐ global governance グローバル・ガバナンス→国境を越えた多様な問題に対応する政治的相互作用
- ☐ successive 歴代の
- ☐ push 推し進める
- ☐ defense capabilities 防衛力
- ☐ diplomacy 外交
- ☐ leading economy 経済大国
- ☐ foreign minister 外務大臣
- ☐ call for ... …を呼び掛ける
- ☐ effective 効果的な
- ☐ representative 代表する
- ☐ organ 組織
- ☐ reaffirm 再度明言する
- ☐ readiness 用意があること
- ☐ take up 引き受ける
- ☐ responsibility 責任
- ☐ contribute 貢献する
- ☐ stability 安定

8   On the sidelines of this week's General Assembly meeting, Mr. Motegi along with counterparts from Germany, India and Brazil —collectively called the Group of Four—issued another call for Security Council reform, in which they confirmed the urgency for change and expressed "disappointment at attempts to derail this process."

`Track 19`

9   Reform is not impossible. The Security Council increased from 11 members to 15 in 1965, with the addition of four nonpermanent members. At that time, the world body had 117 members, up from 51 at its founding. Today, there are 193 members; that growth alone indicates that change is overdue. It is difficult to be optimistic, however. The clock ran out on the anniversary celebrations with 58 countries—nearly one-third of U.N. members—waiting to speak. No date has yet been set for their messages to be heard.

8
- □ on the sidelines of ... …の傍ら
- □ along with ... …とともに
- □ counterpart（職責が）同等である人
- □ collectively 集合的に
- □ the Group of Four G4 諸国→安保理常任理事国入りを目指す、日本、ドイツ、インド、ブラジルの連合
- □ issue 出す
- □ urgency 緊急性
- □ express 表明する
- □ disappointment 失望
- □ attempt 試み
- □ derail 失敗させる、挫折させる

9
- □ impossible 不可能な
- □ member 加盟国
- □ addition 増加
- □ nonpermanent 非常任の
- □ at that time 当時
- □ growth 成長、増加
- □ indicate 示す
- □ overdue 機が熟しきっている
- □ optimistic 楽天的な
- □ run out 尽きる
- □ anniversary celebration 記念式典
- □ nearly …近く
- □ one-third 3分の1
- □ date 日時
- □ yet まだ

A million COVID-19 deaths must drive world to act together

新型コロナの死者数100万人、世界は共同歩調を

October 1, 2020 　　　　　　　　　　●Tracks 20-24 / 訳 pp. 50-51

Track 20

1　This week, the world marked a grim milestone as the 1 millionth death from the COVID-19 pandemic was recorded. The death count grows by several thousand every day. Horrific as that number is, it is likely that the actual death count is much higher. It will certainly grow: Dr. Mike Ryan, head of the emergency program at the World Health Organization (WHO), warns that even 2 million deaths are possible.

2　Those deaths—over 1,500 of which occurred in Japan—are a fraction of the more than 33 million people around the world who have been infected with the disease in the nine months since COVID-19 was first identified in Wuhan, China. For those who survive the infection, life can be limited and painful, with lingering aftereffects that range from the inconvenient to the crippling. Unquantifiable, but no less debilitating are the psychic and psychological suffering that is inflicted. The global community is unlikely to ever know the cost of the loss of human contact, the divided families, uncertainty, fear and in some cases raw hostility that is being generated.

新型コロナウイルス感染症の勢いは収まらず、北半球が冬を迎える中での第二波が懸念される。ワクチン開発までの間、感染拡大を抑えつつ経済・社会活動を維持するためには、政府の難しいかじ取りが求められるが、まずは一人一人の自覚ある行動が必要である。

1
- □ [タイトル]COVID-19 新型コロナウイルス感染症→Coronavirus Disease 2019 の略
- □ grim ぞっとするような
- □ milestone 節目の数字→「マイル標、一里塚」が本来の意味
- □ pandemic パンデミック、(疫病の)世界的大流行
- □ death count 死者数

- □ by several thousand every day 毎日数千人の単位で
- □ horrific 恐ろしい
- □ as →...(形容詞) as で「…だけれども」の意
- □ emergency 緊急
- □ the World Health Organization 世界保健機関

2
- □ fraction ほんの一部
- □ be infected with ... …に感染する
- □ identify 確認する、特定する
- □ infection 感染症
- □ lingering 長引く
- □ aftereffect(s) 後遺症
- □ range from A to B AからBにまで及ぶ
- □ inconvenient 不便な
- □ crippling (体が)不自由な
- □ unquantifiable 数量化できない

- □ no less ... 同じくらい…
- □ debilitating 衰弱させる
- □ psychic 精神的な
- □ psychological 心理的な
- □ suffering 苦痛
- □ inflict 負わせる
- □ be unlikely to *do* 〜しそうもない
- □ divided 分断された
- □ uncertainty 不確かさ
- □ raw hostility むき出しの敵意
- □ generate 生み出す

Track 21

3   The economic impact of this crisis has reached historic proportions; and while not as bad as the Great Depression of the 1930s, it is thought to be about three times worse than the Great Recession of over a decade ago. The World Bank believes that this will be the first time since the Asian Economic Crisis of 1998 that global poverty will rise, with about 500 million people becoming impoverished as a result of the pandemic. In the East Asia and Pacific regions alone, some 38 million people are expected to either remain in, or return to, poverty.

4   Economic impacts vary. Japan, according to the International Monetary Fund (IMF), is expected to experience a decline of 5.8 percent in 2020, with a recovery to 2.4 percent growth in 2021. The IMF predicted that European GDP (including the United Kingdom) will drop by 10.2 percent this year, while the U.S. economy will shrink by 8 percent. The World Bank forecasts that China, the country first hit by the coronavirus, will grow 2.0 percent this year and 7.9 percent in 2021. India, another driver of regional growth but the second hardest-hit country with more than 6 million confirmed cases, is expected to experience a 9 percent contraction this year, before rebounding to 8 percent growth in 2021.

Track 22

5   The rest of East Asia will not fare as well. Those economies are projected to shrink by 3.5 percent this year and then return to 5.1 percent growth in 2021. While any recovery is to be applauded, these numbers are smaller than estimates before the crisis.

3
- □ impact 影響
- □ crisis 危機
- □ proportion 規模
- □ the Great Depression 世界大恐慌
- □ be thought to be ... …であると考えられる
- □ three times worse than ... …よりも3倍ひどい
- □ the Great Recession of over a decade ago →2008年のリーマン・ショックに端を発した金融危機を指す
- □ the World Bank 世界銀行
- □ the Asian Economic Crisis アジア経済危機
- □ poverty 貧困
- □ impoverished 生活に窮した
- □ be expected to *do* ～すると予想される

4
- □ vary さまざまである
- □ according to ... …によると
- □ the International Monetary Fund 国際通貨基金
- □ experience 経験する
- □ decline 下落
- □ recovery 回復
- □ growth 成長
- □ predict 予測する
- □ GDP 国内総生産→gross domestic product の略
- □ shrink 縮小する
- □ forecast 予測する
- □ coronavirus コロナウイルス
- □ driver けん引役、推進力
- □ regional 地域の
- □ second hardest-hit 2番目に大きな打撃を受けた
- □ confirmed 確認された
- □ contraction 縮小
- □ rebound to ... …に回復する

5
- □ fare as well 同じくらいうまくやっていく
- □ be projected to *do* ～すると予測される
- □ applaud 称賛する
- □ estimate 見積もり、推定値

6   Millions of jobs have been lost and lives changed. In many countries, workers are already being hired back but elsewhere the rise in unemployment may be enduring. Unfortunately, many of the hardest-hit countries are least able to cushion the blows, lacking social safety nets. The current crisis has pushed those governments, historically stingy, to do more. The World Bank, for its part, applauds regional governments that have committed nearly 5 percent of their GDP to public health and support for households and companies during the pandemic. This is in their self-interest: Experts and economists fear that without remedial measures, COVID-19 could depress East Asia's growth over the next 10 years by 1 percentage point a year.

Track 23

7   As debilitating as those losses are, and equally disruptive over time, is the damage that the outbreak has done to international relations. It is too early to say if COVID-19 will lead to a permanent shift in the global balance of power—much depends on whether the United States, where over 200,000 lives have been lost, gets control of the situation and regains its status as a trusted leader committed to cooperative, multilateral solutions. The fumbling response from the U.S.—20 percent of all deaths despite just 4 percent of the global population — has done great damage to its standing and image in the world. U.S. President Donald Trump has preferred to blame China for his country's misfortunes and to penalize the WHO for putting cooperation above name calling.

6
- ☐ be hired back 再雇用される
- ☐ unemployment 失業（率）
- ☐ enduring 長続きする
- ☐ be least able to *do* 最も～できそうにない
- ☐ cushion 緩和する
- ☐ blow 打撃
- ☐ social safety net 社会的セーフティーネット→事故や失業などでの困窮時の生活保障制度
- ☐ current 現在の

- ☐ historically 歴史的に
- ☐ stingy けちな
- ☐ commit A to B AをBに付する
- ☐ public health 公衆衛生
- ☐ household 世帯
- ☐ self-interest 自己の利益
- ☐ expert 専門家
- ☐ economist 経済学者
- ☐ remedial measure(s) 救済策
- ☐ depress 押し下げる

7
- ☐ disruptive 壊滅的な
- ☐ over time 時間とともに
- ☐ outbreak （疫病の）大流行
- ☐ lead to ... …につながる、…を引き起こす
- ☐ permanent 恒久的な
- ☐ shift 変化
- ☐ balance of power 勢力バランス
- ☐ depend on whether ... …かどうかにかかっている
- ☐ get control of ... …を制御する
- ☐ situation 状況
- ☐ regain 取り戻す
- ☐ status 地位

- ☐ cooperative 協調的な
- ☐ multilateral 多国間の
- ☐ fumbling ぎこちない
- ☐ response 対応
- ☐ despite …にもかかわらず
- ☐ population 人口
- ☐ standing 地位
- ☐ prefer to *do* ～することを好む
- ☐ blame A for B AをBのことで責める
- ☐ misfortune 災難、不幸
- ☐ penalize 罰する
- ☐ put A above B AをBよりも優先する
- ☐ cooperation 協調
- ☐ name calling 誹謗中傷、悪口

8   Few leaders and governments have acquitted themselves well. But the nature of any pandemic threat and the connections of the global economy—whether the specific vaccine and personal protective equipment supply chains or the general linkages that ensure its smooth function in normal times—demand coordinated transnational responses. To date, the world has failed.

Track 24

9   There will be a second chance. COVID-19 is gaining traction in the southern hemisphere and second waves are swelling in countries in Europe and Asia. Some experts believe that Japan experienced that surge in August. The U.S. is bracing for a second wave as well. The basic steps that individuals must take are known: wearing masks, social distancing, washing hands. Governments must look at the big picture: testing, contact tracing, quarantining and preparing their societies for economic and social hardships while doing their best to cushion the hardships. Japan should be supporting and driving diplomacy—while ensuring that it follows best practices at home.

8
- ☐ acquit *oneself* well 自分の義務を果たす
- ☐ nature 本質
- ☐ threat 脅威
- ☐ specific 具体的な
- ☐ vaccine ワクチン
- ☐ personal protective equipment 個人用防護具→マスク、手袋など
- ☐ supply chain サプライチェーン
- ☐ linkage つながり
- ☐ ensure 確実にする
- ☐ coordinated 協調的な
- ☐ transnational 国を超えた
- ☐ to date 現在までのところ

9
- ☐ gain traction 勢いを増す
- ☐ southern hemisphere 南半球
- ☐ second wave 第二波
- ☐ swell 増大する
- ☐ that surge その高まり→第二波のこと
- ☐ brace for ... …に備える
- ☐ individual 個人
- ☐ social distancing ソーシャルディスタンスを取ること
- ☐ look at the big picture 大局的な視点から見る
- ☐ contact tracing 接触者の追跡
- ☐ quarantining 隔離すること
- ☐ hardship 苦難
- ☐ diplomacy 外交
- ☐ practice 慣習

A return to normalcy as the Biden administration emerges

バイデン政権誕生で米国は正常復帰へ

November 26, 2020 　　　　　　　　●Tracks 25-30 / 訳 pp. 52-54

Track 25

1　This week, U.S. President-elect Joe Biden announced the nominees for his national security team. All are familiar faces, experts in their fields, with extensive experience in the bureaucracies that they will soon lead.

2　It is a capable and competent group, one that will serve U.S. national interests and reassure allies that the new administration understands its roles and responsibilities and takes them seriously. The rest of the world and the Republican opposition may not cooperate in that endeavor, however, and whatever return to normalcy that candidate Biden promised may prove beyond his and his team's reach.

Track 26

3　First and most important, it is composed of foreign policy traditionalists who believe that the U.S. must be engaged in the world, endeavor to lead and should do so through the multilateral institutions that previous administrations worked so hard to build. Their instincts are to consult and do so first with allies and longtime partners.

4　Second, they are close to the president-elect. Foreign leaders must know that envoys with whom they meet speak for the president, and that their words are his words. Nothing is more damaging to an emissary's effectiveness than the perception of a gap between the president and his representative. Diplomats in the Trump

バイデン次期米大統領により安全保障関連の人事が発表された。実務経験者・専門家ぞろいで、大統領との連携も密な顔ぶれである。西側同盟国を主導する方針を採る新政権の形がはっきりしてくるにつれ、バイデン氏が公約した「正常への復帰」が見えてきたようだ。

1
- [タイトル]normalcy 正常、常態
- [タイトル]administration 政権
- [タイトル]emerge 姿を現す
- president-elect 次期大統領
- nominee 候補者
- national security 国家安全保障
- extensive 幅広い
- bureaucracy 官僚組織

2
- capable 有能な
- competent 有能な、適任である
- reassure 安心させる
- ally 同盟国
- responsibility 責任
- rest 残り
- Republican 共和党の
- opposition 反対勢力
- cooperate 協力する
- endeavor 努力、試み
- candidate 候補者
- prove (…であることが)判明する、わかる
- beyond *one's* reach 〜の手が届かない

3
- first and most important まず最も重要なことには
- be composed of ... …で構成される
- foreign policy 外交政策
- traditionalist 伝統主義者
- be engaged in ... …に関与する
- lead 主導する
- multilateral institution 多国間機関
- previous 以前の
- build 構築する
- instinct 本能
- consult 相談する
- longtime 長年の

4
- envoy 特使
- speak for ... …を代弁する
- damaging 損害を与える
- emissary 特使、使節
- effectiveness 効果、有効性
- perception 認識
- gap 落差、溝
- representative 代理人
- diplomat 外交官

administration, no matter how senior or what the mission, were often undercut by presidential pronouncements that conflicted with the messages that they were trying to deliver, even if only minutes or hours apart.

Track 27

5 There is in the Biden team a consistency of views between principal and agents, as well as respect for the policymaking process. There will be no freelancing by Biden officials, because they know what the president wants and appreciate the relationship between ends and means.

6 There are two dangers for the new administration. The first is overconfidence. This group knows their jobs; some were in similar positions just four years ago. The world has changed since then, however, and the Biden team must grasp and respond to that evolution. The president-elect acknowledged this new reality when he announced the nominations, explaining that "While this team has unmatched experience and accomplishments, they also reflect the idea that we cannot meet these challenges with old thinking and unchanged habits." Central to this assignment are changes in the way that alliances operate and are managed.

Track 28

7 Success demands recognition that the populism behind Mr. Trump's "America First" policies has not dissipated. Foreign policy must better serve the interests of the middle class and not be seen as a tool of elites. National Security Advisor Jake Sullivan knows this well: He served on a task force that focused on this issue. He must ensure that the Biden administration puts that understanding to use if its policies are to be sustainable.

□ no matter how ... どんなに…であろうと
□ senior 古参の、先輩の
□ mission 任務
□ undercut 効果をなくす

□ pronouncement 宣言
□ conflict with ... …と矛盾する、相いれない、食い違う
□ deliver 伝える
□ apart 離れて

5
□ consistency 一貫性
□ view(s) 見解
□ principal 主導者
□ agent 代理人
□ policymaking process 政策決定の過程

□ freelancing 一匹おおかみとして行動すること
□ official 官僚、当局者
□ appreciate 正しく認識する
□ relationship 関係
□ ends and means 目的と手段

6
□ overconfidence 過信
□ similar 同じような
□ position 職務、地位
□ grasp 把握する
□ respond 応じる
□ evolution 進展、進化
□ acknowledge 認める
□ reality 現実
□ nomination 指名
□ unmatched 比類のない

□ accomplishment 実績、業績
□ reflect 反映する
□ meet …をうまく処理する
□ habit 慣習
□ central to ... …の中心となる→この文では主語と補語が倒置されている
□ assignment 任務
□ alliance 同盟
□ operate 機能する
□ manage 管理する、運営する

7
□ populism ポピュリズム、大衆迎合主義
□ "America First" policies 「米国第一」政策
□ dissipate 消散する
□ interest(s) 利益
□ middle class 中間層、中産階級
□ tool 道具
□ National Security Advisor 国家安全保障担当補佐官

□ task force 対策委員会
□ focus on ... …に焦点を絞る
□ issue 問題
□ ensure 確実にする、保証する
□ put ... to use …を役立てる、利用する
□ understanding 理解
□ sustainable 持続可能な

8   That logic dictates a more expansive definition of national security, one that the Trump administration has adopted—and perhaps taken beyond its proper limit. Policymakers must better operationalize the connection between economic and national security. Japan has been moving in this direction with the reorganization of the National Security Council and National Security Secretariat. In the U.S. case, it means that the attorney general and the secretaries of Treasury and Commerce will play vital roles in a world in which the competition among great powers is multidimensional.

`Track 29`

9   The main competitor is China and U.S. allies in Asia (and increasingly in Europe) will be called upon to join efforts to end Chinese misbehavior and contain the spread of Beijing's influence. China policy will be one of the most important tests of the new administration's seriousness and credibility, and there will be laser-like scrutiny of issues where it is prepared to engage with China. Mr. Biden cannot sacrifice or compromise its allies' national interests for a deal on another set of concerns.

10   Japan will be especially attentive to the role played by John Kerry, a longtime friend of Mr. Biden who has been named international climate envoy. Climate change was Mr. Kerry's signature issue when he served as Barack Obama's second secretary of state, and he was the chief U.S. negotiator for the Paris climate accord, a deal that Mr. Trump withdrew from after six months in office. Climate change is a serious threat and it cannot be solved without China's participation, but Japanese equities cannot be sacrificed in the process. The same is true when dealing with North Korea, Taiwan or Iran.

8
- ☐ logic 論理
- ☐ dictate 必然的に決める、規定する
- ☐ expansive 広範囲の
- ☐ definition 定義
- ☐ adopt 採用する
- ☐ proper 適切な
- ☐ policymaker 政策決定者
- ☐ operationalize 運用可能にする
- ☐ connection つながり、結び付き
- ☐ direction 方向
- ☐ reorganization 再編成
- ☐ the National Security Council 国家安全保障会議
- ☐ National Security Secretariat 国家安全保障局
- ☐ attorney general 司法長官
- ☐ secretaries of Treasury and Commerce 財務長官と商務長官
- ☐ vital 極めて重要な
- ☐ competition 競争
- ☐ great power 大国
- ☐ multidimensional 多次元の

9
- ☐ competitor 競争相手
- ☐ increasingly ますます
- ☐ call upon ... to *do* …に～するよう求める
- ☐ effort 取り組み
- ☐ misbehavior 不正行為
- ☐ contain 封じ込める、阻止する
- ☐ spread 広がり
- ☐ Beijing 中国政府
- ☐ influence 影響
- ☐ seriousness 真剣さ
- ☐ credibility 信頼性
- ☐ laser-like (集中力が) 高い
- ☐ scrutiny 精査
- ☐ sacrifice 犠牲にする
- ☐ compromise 損なう
- ☐ concern 懸案の問題

10
- ☐ especially 特に
- ☐ attentive よく注意している
- ☐ name 任命する
- ☐ climate envoy 気候特使
- ☐ climate change 気候変動
- ☐ signature 特徴的な
- ☐ secretary of state 国務長官
- ☐ chief U.S. negotiator 米首席交渉官
- ☐ Paris climate accord パリ気候協定
  →気候変動に関する国際的枠組み「パリ協定」のこと
- ☐ deal 取り決め、協定
- ☐ withdraw 離脱する
- ☐ in office 在職して
- ☐ threat 脅威
- ☐ solve 解決する
- ☐ participation 参加
- ☐ equity 正当な権利

Track 30

11 The second danger the Biden administration faces concerns the Republican Party. Will it work with the new president to overcome national challenges, such as the COVID-19 outbreak and the recession it has triggered, or will the GOP try to sabotage the new administration by refusing to confirm nominations, undermining efforts to deal with those challenges and launch endless investigations to cripple and distract the government? Mr. Biden believes that he can govern from the center and that the GOP will join him; recent history offers little grounds for optimism. Florida Sen. Marco Rubio, who has aspirations to run for president in 2024, confirmed that skepticism is in order when he judged Mr. Biden's new team to have "strong résumés ... and will be polite and orderly caretakers of America's decline," but added that "I have no interest in returning to the 'normal' that left us dependent on China."

12 Few do, in Washington or in Tokyo. The challenge is building an administration and using it to pursue credible and consistent policies that marshal U.S. and allies' resources to sustain a peaceful and prosperous world. It looks like Mr. Biden has made a good start.

11
- ☐ face 直面する
- ☐ overcome 打ち勝つ、乗り越える
- ☐ COVID-19 新型コロナウイルス感染症 → Coronavirus Disease 2019 の略
- ☐ outbreak （疫病の）大流行
- ☐ recession 不景気
- ☐ trigger 引き起こす
- ☐ the GOP 共和党 → Grand Old Party の頭文字で、米共和党の別称
- ☐ sabotage 妨害行為をする
- ☐ refuse 拒否する
- ☐ confirm 承認する、確認する
- ☐ undermine 傷付ける
- ☐ launch 始める
- ☐ endless 果てしのない
- ☐ investigation 調査
- ☐ cripple 損なう、駄目にする
- ☐ distract 邪魔をする
- ☐ govern 統治する
- ☐ history 経緯
- ☐ offer 提供する
- ☐ ground(s) 根拠
- ☐ optimism 楽観
- ☐ Sen. 上院議員 → senator の略
- ☐ aspiration 強い願望
- ☐ skepticism 疑念、懐疑的な態度
- ☐ in order 適切で
- ☐ résumé 履歴書
- ☐ orderly 整然とした
- ☐ caretaker （職務の一時的な）代行機関
- ☐ decline 衰退
- ☐ leave A B A を B のままにしておく
- ☐ dependent 依存している、頼っている

12
- ☐ few （否定的に）非常に少数の人々
- ☐ Washington 米政府
- ☐ Tokyo 日本政府
- ☐ pursue 追求する、達成しようとする
- ☐ credible 確かな、当てになる
- ☐ consistent 首尾一貫した、堅実な
- ☐ marshal まとめる、集結させる
- ☐ resource(s) 資源
- ☐ sustain 維持する
- ☐ prosperous 繁栄している

世界のてっぺんでの危険な緊張が再燃

1 インドと中国の間の緊張が再び高まっている。今年の夏、ヒマラヤ地方の係争中の国境である実効支配線沿いのラダックで二国の軍が衝突した。30人を超える死者を出したことで両国政府は冷静さを取り戻し、軍事交渉が始まったものの、ほとんど進展は見られなかった。先月下旬、二国の軍の間で再度の衝突が発生し、それは幸いなことに物理的な形ではなく言葉によるものではあったが、停戦のもろさを強調することとなった。

2 敵意はより広い関係にも波及している。両国の国民は相手にますます敵対心を募らせており、インド政府は北の隣国に対して経済的な攻勢を仕かけた。どちらの国も国家主義者がトップに立っているため、さらなる衝突と事態の拡大の可能性が現実味を帯びている。

3 インドと中国は3,500キロに及ぶ国境の実効支配線をめぐって、長年にわたり争ってきた。1962年には紛争になり(このときはインドが敗北したが)、その後も何度か衝突を繰り返してきた。事態が深刻化する可能性があったことから、両国は1993年に交戦規定を受け入れ、双方が国境警備隊の火器の使用を禁止した。

4 それが効力を持っていたのは、この6月に両国が互いに相手の領土侵犯を非難するまでのことだった。双方から数百人の兵士が動員され、6月半ばのある夜、小競り合いになった。銃火器の使用はなかったものの死者は出た。兵士たちは石、木切れ、こん棒、素手で争い、1970年代以降で初めて、人命が失われた。数十人の兵士が命を落とし(中国は自軍の死傷者を一切認めなかったが)十数人のインド軍兵士が人質に取られた(そして、のちに解放されている)。

5 それ以来、その傷口が膿んだような状態が続いていて、特にインド国民の間ではそうであった。インド軍はもはや古い交戦規定には従わないと述べた。7月初め、インドのナレンドラ・モディ首相はほかの政府高官とともにラダックを訪問し、兵士たちへの支援とインフラ支出の約束を申し出たが、いずれもこの問題に関する首相の懸念を中国政府に示したものだった。

6 数回に及ぶ交渉の末、つい2週間前、両国政府は「迅速な方法」で、かつ既存の協定に従って問題を解決することに合意した。インドの外務省は、「実効支配線沿いの兵士の完全な撤退に向けて、双方が真摯に取り組み続ける」と確約する声明を発表した。

7 その報道から数日後、両国が同地域にさらなる兵士を派遣し、防備を固めているとのニュースが入った。インドは中国が紛争地域に監視台、掩蔽壕、係留地点を建設していると非難し、そうした活動は「以前の合意に違反する」もので、「挑発的な軍事行動」に等しいと語った。両国の部隊は1メートル以内の距離に近づき、怒鳴り合いになった後に引き離されたと言われている。インド特殊部隊のチベット族隊員が1人、中国の部隊との紛争再発現場の近くで地雷の爆発により死亡した。

8 中国外交部の報道官によると、中国軍は「決して実効支配線を越えることはない」とのことである。中国人民解放軍の報道官は、実効支配線を越えるという「あからさまな挑発行為」があったとして、インド軍を非難した。言葉を並べるばかりの自己防衛は、インドの主張する「お互いに合意した歩み寄り」の余地を狭めている。

9 増大しつつある兵士の駐留が、再度の武力衝突の可能性を現実的なものにしている。その傾向は、モディ首相が6月の事件の深刻さを当初は軽視し、その処理を誤ったとの認識によって強まっている。インド政府高官、特に軍関係者は、中国が現状を変更していると主張し、軍事的な膠着状態に対応する手順に幻滅している。

10 中国の戦略家は、インドが保有する領土で、パキスタンもその領有を主張するジャンムー・カシミール州の地位を変更し、ラダックをそこから分離させて連邦直轄領として統治するという昨年のインド政府の決定を指摘して、インドこそが修正主義者だと反論している。彼らにしてみれば、その決定には中国側からの反応があって当然であった。

11 インドは自国経済への中国のアクセスを制限する対策を採用し、第二戦線に向かって進んでいる。最初の衝突の前でさえ、インドは中国からの投資すべてに対して政府の認可が必要であると規則を変更していた。その後は投資の制限をさらに厳格化し、中国からの広範囲に及ぶ輸入品に関税を課し、180本近い中国製のアプリを禁止し、地元の電気通信事業者に対してはファーウェイやZTEといった中国企業の機器の使用を段階的に廃止するように伝えた。

12 インドの総輸入額に占める中国の割合は、2000年の3%未満から2018年には14%と4倍以上に増えており、制限は双方に損害を与えることとなるが、多くの消費者が「中国ボイコット」運動を支持している中でインドの国民感情は硬化してきている。中国でも同様に怒りの声が高まりつつある。8月に環球時報が実施した世論調査によると、70%超の中国国民はインドが中国に対して敵対的すぎると考えており、90%近くが中国政府による「インドの挑発行為への報復」を支持している。

世界のてっぺんでの危険な緊張が再燃

13 国家主義的な指導者、敵対的な国民、軍事衝突、核武装した隣国同士。これは考えうる限りの危険極まりない組み合わせである。外交と首脳レベルによる仲介がますます急を要しているが、パンデミックという状況でそれはますます困難になっている。相互の配置転換と両国軍による撤退のためのメンツを保てる解決策が、欠かすことのできない第一歩である。　　　　　　　　　　　（訳・注　桑田）

毒殺未遂疑惑があらわにしたプーチン大統領の世界

1 ロシアのウラジーミル・プーチン大統領の政権が犯した暴挙は数多く、そのリストは長大化している。最も新しい出来事は野党党首アレクセイ・ナワリヌイ氏の毒物襲撃疑惑で、彼は先月ロシアで旅客機に搭乗した際に具合が悪くなった。ナワリヌイ氏は治療のためドイツに搬送され、そこでの検査で神経ガスが使われていたことが判明した。ロシア政府は疑惑を否定しているが、証拠と論理がそうした非難の裏付けになっている。これらのことを踏まえて、国際社会はこの野蛮な行為に対して形式的な非難声明を再々出す以上のことをすべきだ。従来通りの外交ではそうした蛮行を助長するだけだろう。

2 ナワリヌイ氏はロシアで最も注目を浴びている反体制派指導者である。10年超にわたって政府と与党の組織的な汚職を糾弾し、その活動は各地に根付いていった。これまでに13回投獄され、横領罪で6年の実刑判決を受けた。ナワリヌイ氏は、これらの嫌疑は自分を沈黙させるための口実だったと主張している。この有罪判決は、プーチン大統領の対立候補として選挙に出馬することを禁じているのだ。

3 どうやら、出馬阻止だけでは十分ではなかったようで、それよりも、ナワリヌイ氏を黙らせる必要があった。シベリアからモスクワに向かう機内で、ナワリヌイ氏は体調がひどく悪化し、旅客機はオムスク市への方向転換を余儀なくされて、彼はそこで入院した。妻や支援者の懇願にもかかわらず、ロシア当局は彼が治療のためにドイツへ移送されることを認めようとせず、その決定は3日後にようやく覆され、彼はベルリン行きを許された。

4 ドイツの医師と化学兵器の専門家らは、旧ソ連時代に開発された神経ガスのノビチョクがナワリヌイ氏に盛られたという「明白な証拠」を検査が示していると言う。しかし、オムスク市のロシア医師団が毒物の形跡を見つけられなかったことに言及して、ロシアはこの主張を否定し、ドイツ政府に検査結果の共有を求めている。

5 ドイツ政府はその要求に応じるべきだが、それはロシアにとっては大して重要なことではないだろう。ロシア政府は、あらゆる手段を用いていかなる場所でも反対派の口を封じる準備ができていることを隠し立てしていない。反体制派毒殺の試みは過去5年間、ロシア国内で数回、国外で数回の少なくとも6回起きた。ナワリヌイ氏は収監時に一度、毒を盛られたことがあると言う。今回は旅客機に搭乗する前に空港で飲んだお茶に毒を入れられたと見られている。

毒殺未遂疑惑があらわにしたプーチン大統領の世界

6　ノビチョクは冷戦時代にソ連によって開発・兵器化された強力な神経ガスである。その存在は亡命ロシア人によって明らかにされたが、化学兵器禁止条約に基づいてロシアの化学兵器備蓄が廃棄された際、ロシア政府はノビチョクを一度も申告していなかった。ノビチョクを開発したことで知られている国はほかになく、またその生産工程の複雑さが意味しているのは、所有が可能なのは政府だけであろうということだ。

7　同様に罪を明らかにする事実として、ノビチョクは 2018 年に英国で、元ロシア側のスパイであったセルゲイ・スクリパリ氏とその娘の攻撃に使用されたのであった。その事件では 6 人が中毒症状を起こした。そのうちの一人（スクリパリ氏ではない）は香水瓶を拾った後に死亡しており、その瓶は毒物を運ぶのに使われた後、不用意に捨てられたものだった。ノビチョクの出所や、ロシア政府が敵視している人物への使用、そしてそうした疑惑の話になるときのロシアの無関心さ、そのすべてがロシア政府の関与を裏付けている。

8　この最後の点が最も決定的であり、それに対する強い対策が求められる。ロシア政府は、敵を黙らせるためにはどんな一線も越えるし、誰にも止められないと心得ている。そう考える以外に、元スパイでロシア政府の批判者だったアレクサンドル・リトビネンコ氏を 2006 年に殺害するためにポロニウムが使われたことを説明できない。その毒物から発せられた放射線は容易に追跡できる痕跡を残し、殺害者たちがどこに滞在し、どこで食事をしたか、ロシアからの往復で搭乗した旅客機、さらには機中で座った席まで示していた。

9　各国政府と欧州連合（EU）は、ナワリヌイ事件に関してロシア政府による調査を要求したが、それだけでは不十分だ。主要 7 カ国（G7）は今週、外相らがナワリヌイ氏への「確認された毒物の使用を可能な限り最も強い表現で非難」するという第一歩を踏み出したが、「恐ろしい毒物使用」に関する説明を求める呼び掛けにロシアがどう反応するか「注視する」という誓約は弱腰に思われる。

10　ロシアはその殺人行為を罰せられ、プーチン大統領から自身が無敵であるという思い込みを剥ぎ取るべきだ。いつも通りであってはならない。欧州はロシアからのガスを供給するパイプライン「ノルドストリーム 2」に対する姿勢を見直すべきだ。かつては聖域とされていたその事業について、ドイツの外相は今となっては検討もありうると示唆した。ドイツのアンゲラ・メルケル首相も同意を示している。フラン

スは政府の怒りの表明として、外相と国防相による念願だったモスクワ訪問を延期した。

11 今回の殺人行為はロシア国内で起きたのだから、他国にできることは限られていると考えたいという誘惑に駆られる。それは間違っている。ロシアが国境を重視していることを示す証拠は何もない。法律などお構いなく、どこであろうと望む場所で思うままに行動してきた。このことは日本ほかすべての政府にとって、ロシアおよびプーチン大統領との取引を考えるときに最も注意すべき点である。

（訳・注　宇都宮）

ダイヤモンド・ジュビリーを迎えても輝けない国連

1　ダイヤモンド・ジュビリー（75年祭）は、事前録画の演説よりましな方法で祝うべき
ものだが、ほぼ空っぽの総会議場で放映された3分間演説ビデオの羅列は、何らか
の形で国連の現状を端的にとらえている。世界は現代史上例のない一連の危機（新
型コロナウイルス感染症の世界的大流行、混迷した世界経済、気候災害）に直面
しており、国連は、地政学的な敵対意識や、各国政府が国連機関の無策に不満を
こぼす一方で、独自行動に走る傾向を強めていることに悩まされている。アントニ
オ・グテーレス国連事務総長が国連の創設75周年記念式典での発言の中で説明し
たように、「多国間の問題は有り余っているが、多国間の解決策は不足している」。

2　これは「1945年の再現」だと、グテーレス事務総長は警告した。新型コロナの大
流行は「世界の脆弱さを露呈させた。……気候災害が迫り、生物多様性は崩壊し
つつあり、貧困は増加し、憎しみは広がり、地政学的緊張は高まり、核兵器はい
まだに即時発射の態勢にある」。それなのに、この危機的な状況下でさえ協調行
動には手が届かない。

3　至るところから非難の声が上がっている。米国は実質的に国連に肘鉄を食らわせ
た。ドナルド・トランプ米大統領は、月曜日の記念式典で式辞を述べる182の国・
政府首脳の筆頭に挙げられていたにもかかわらず、おそれ多くもお話しになること
はなく、代わりに国連次席大使代理を派遣し、その大使代理は、国連はあまりに
も長く「意義ある改革」に抵抗しており、透明性に欠け、「専制国家や独裁国家の
意向にあまりにも影響を受けやすい」と不満を述べた。

4　いざ国連に向けて話をするとなると、トランプ氏はその週の後半、国連総会への
短い事前録画演説の中でけんか腰の態度を見せた。「中国ウイルス…この疫病」を
世界に向けて解き放ったとして、トランプ氏は中国を攻撃した。また、パリの気候
協定とイラン核合意を非難し、昨年もやったことだが、自分の「米国第一」政策を
見習うようほかの国々に呼び掛けた。

5　中国の習近平国家主席、ロシアのウラジーミル・プーチン大統領のような他国の首
脳たちは、そのような考え方を拒否して多国間主義と協調を受け入れるよう、各国
に呼び掛けたが、重要なのは言葉と行為を一致させることだ。両氏は自分たちとト
ランプ氏とを対比させること（自分たちを簡単によく見せるやり方）を楽しんでいる
が、国家特権を守るということになるとトランプ氏同様、かたくなに譲ろうとせず、
問題との取り組みにおいては同じくらい妨害者であり、国連改革への意欲のなさに

かけても米国に劣らず、場合によっては米国以上にそうすることを渋ってきた。

6　改革の取り組みの焦点は、中国、フランス、ロシア、米国、英国の5カ国が常任議席と審議の拒否権を持っている、安全保障理事会である。その議席は、第二次世界大戦の戦勝国としての国の地位を反映したものだったが、以後75年間のうちに世界は変貌し、そうした国々の力と特権はもはや国際的現実を反映していない。にもかかわらず、その国々の政府は自分の力を失うことを意味するなら、組織の近代化を拒否する。彼らにとって同様に重みを持つのが、競争相手が台頭してくる可能性だ。中国政府には、それぞれ地域の主導権を競う相手である日本もインドも安保理に入れる気がない。ロシア政府は、ドイツにそういう地位や権力を与えるという考えを快く思っていない。中国とロシアの拒否権は、改革が進展しないことを意味する。（インドの場合はパキスタン、ドイツの場合はイタリアといった地域において比較的規模の小さい競争相手も、やはり改革に反対している）

7　国連創設時に明示された展望に、日本はこれからも積極的に関わっていく。それは共通の目的のために結束した世界、すなわち、戦争の防止、法の支配および紛争の平和的解決の促進、そして、人権およびすべての国民が繁栄し、健康であり、グローバル・ガバナンスに参加できるよう機会均等を保証することである。歴代の日本政府は、防衛力の向上を推し進めつつも、外交や多国間主義を推進し、国際機関を通じて世界が抱える課題に引き続き取り組んでいる。日本が国連を改革しようとする動きは、より多くを成し遂げたいという願いを反映しており、それは世界第3位の経済国としては当然だ。記念式典での発言で、茂木敏充外相は21世紀の世界の「効果的かつ代表的な組織」にするために、国連安全保障理事会の改革を呼び掛けた。茂木外相は、日本が国連安保理常任理事国の責任を引き受ける用意があることと、「世界の平和と安定の確保に貢献すること」を再び明言した。

8　今週行われた総会の傍ら、茂木外相はドイツ、インド、ブラジル（合わせてG4諸国と呼ばれる）の外相とともに安保理改革を再度打ち出して、改変が急務であることを確認し、また、「この工程をくじこうとする試みへの失望」も表明した。

9　改革は不可能ではない。安全保障理事会は、1965年に非常任理事国4国が加わって、11カ国から15カ国に拡大した。当時、創設時の51カ国から増加して117カ国が国連に加盟していた。今日の加盟国は193カ国だ。この成長からだけでも、変革の機がすでに熟していることがわかる。しかし、楽観的になるのは難しい。58カ国（国連加盟国の3分の1近く）が演説をしようと待っていた中、記念式典は時間切れとなった。それらの国々のメッセージを聞く日付は、まだ設定されていない。
　　　　　　　　　　　　　　　　　　　　　　　　　　　　　（訳・注　中村）

新型コロナの死者数100万人、世界は共同歩調を

1　今週、新型コロナウイルス感染症（COVID-19）のパンデミックでの100万人目の死者が記録され、世界はぞっとするような節目の数字に到達した。死者数は毎日数千人の単位で増加している。その数字も恐ろしいが、実際の死者数ははるかに多いと考えられる。今後も間違いなく増えるであろう。世界保健機関（WHO）の緊急対応責任者のマイク・ライアン博士は、200万人の死者数の可能性すらあると警鐘を鳴らした。

2　死者数（そのうちの1,500人超は日本における数字だが）は、中国の武漢でCOVID-19が最初に確認されてから9カ月の間に病気に感染した全世界の3300万人以上のうちの、ほんの一部にすぎない。感染症を克服した人でも、ちょっとした不便から体の不自由にまで及ぶ長引く後遺症のせいで、生活が制限されて苦痛を伴うものになる可能性がある。数字では表せないものの、同じように体を衰弱させるのが、精神的および心理的な負担となる苦痛である。国際社会は、人間同士の触れ合いの喪失、分断された家族、不確かさ、恐怖、また、場合によっては引き起こされているむき出しの敵意による損失を、計り知ることはないであろう。

3　今回の危機の経済的な影響は歴史的な規模に達した。1930年代の大恐慌ほどはひどくないものの、10年以上前の世界金融危機のおよそ3倍のひどさだと考えられている。世界銀行は1998年のアジア経済危機以降で初めて、世界の貧困が増えると見ていて、パンデミックの結果として約5億人が生活に窮するとされる。東アジアと太平洋地域だけでも、3800万人余りが貧しい状態にとどまる、もしくは戻ると予想されている。

4　経済的な影響はさまざまである。国際通貨基金（IMF）によると、日本は2020年に（成長率が）5.8%のマイナスになり、2021年は2.4%の成長に回復すると予想されている。IMFは、ヨーロッパ（英国を含む）のGDPが今年は10.2%下落し、一方で、米国経済は8%縮小すると予測する。世界銀行は、コロナウイルスに最初に見舞われた中国は、今年2.0%、2021年は7.9%成長すると予想している。もう一つの地域経済成長の担い手ながら、600万人以上の患者が確認されて世界で2番目に大きな打撃を受けているインドは、今年は9%の縮小を経た後、2021年には8%の成長に回復すると予想されている。

5　そのほかの東アジアはそれほど見通しがよくない。それらの国々の経済は、今年が3.5%の縮小、2021年には5.1%の成長に戻ると予測される。いかなる回復でも称

賛されるべきものだとはいえ、こうした数字は危機以前の見積もりと比べると小さい。

6 数百万人分の仕事が失われ、生活が一変した。多くの国々では、すでに労働者が再雇用されているが、失業率の上昇が長続きしそうなところもある。残念なことに、最も大きな打撃を受けた国々の多くは、社会的セーフティーネットが欠けていて、打撃を緩和する能力が最も低い。現在の危機は、これまで歴史的に財政支出を渋ってきたそうした国々の政府にもっと支出するように強いている。世界銀行の側は、パンデミックの間にGDPの5%近く(の資金)を公衆衛生や世帯および企業の支援に投入した地方政府を称賛している。これは自分たちの利益にかなうものだ。専門家や経済学者は、救済策がなければ、COVID−19は今後10年間の東アジアの成長率を年に1%分、押し下げるのではないかと不安視している。

7 そうした損失と同じくらい衰弱をもたらし、時とともに同様に壊滅的になったのは、感染の流行が国際関係にもたらしたダメージである。COVID−19が世界の勢力バランスの恒久的な変化につながるかどうかを判断するのは時期尚早だ。多くは、20万人を超す死者を出した米国が状況を制御し、協調的かつ多国間での解決策に取り組む信頼できるリーダーとしての地位を取り戻せるか否かにかかっている。人口は世界の4%にもかかわらず、総死者数の20%を占める米国のまずい対応は、世界におけるその地位とイメージに大きなダメージを与えた。米国のドナルド・トランプ大統領は、自国の災難の責任は中国にあると非難したり、悪口を言うよりも協調を優先したWHOを罰したりするほうを選んできた。

8 ほとんどの指導者や政府は自分の職責を果たしていない。しかし、パンデミックというものの脅威の本質や、世界経済の結び付き(それが、具体的なワクチンや個人用防護具のサプライチェーンであろうと、あるいは平常時におけるその円滑な機能を保証する総合的なつながりであろうと)には、国を超えた協調的な対応が要求される。現在までのところ、世界はそれができていない。

9 2度目のチャンスがあるだろう。COVID−19は南半球で勢いを増しており、ヨーロッパやアジアの国々では第二波のうねりが高まりつつある。日本は8月にその高まりを経験したと考える専門家もいる。米国も第二波の襲来に備えている。個人が取らなければならない基本的な対策は周知されている。マスクを着用すること、ソーシャルディスタンスを取ること、手洗いをすることである。政府は大局的な視点から見なければならない。検査、接触者の追跡、隔離、さらには、経済的および社会的苦難に自らの社会を備えさせる一方で、その苦難の緩和に最善を尽くすことである。日本は外交を支援し、けん引するべきであるが、ここでもはやり、国内では最善の習慣をしっかりと守らなければならない。　　　　(訳・注　桑田)

バイデン政権誕生で米国は正常復帰へ

1 今週、ジョー・バイデン次期米大統領は、国家安全保障チームの候補者を発表した。全員よく知られた顔ぶれであり、それぞれの分野の専門家で、近いうちに率いることになる官僚組織において広範な経験を持っている。

2 これは才能があり適任な集団で、米国の国益のために尽くし、また新政権が自らの役割と責任を理解しており、かつ真摯に受け止めているとして同盟国を安心させるものだ。とはいえ、世界のほかの国々や野党共和党は、その取り組みに協力しないかもしれないし、バイデン候補が約束した正常への復帰なるものは、バイデン氏とそのチームの手の届かないところにあると判明するかもしれない。

3 まず最も重要なのは、このチームが外交政策の伝統主義者たちで構成されており、彼らが米国は世界に関与して、けん引に努めなければならず、それを歴代の米政権が懸命に構築してきた多国間機関を通じて行うべきだと信じていることだ。彼らの本能は相談すること、まずそれを、同盟国や長年のパートナーから始めることである。

4 第二に、彼らは次期大統領に近しい。外国の指導者は、自分が会う特使は大統領の代弁者であり、その言葉は大統領の言葉であると心得るべきだ。大統領とその代弁者との間にずれがあるという認識ほど、特使の有効性を損なうものはない。トランプ政権の外交官は、いかに古参であれ、任務が何であれ、たとえほんの数分もしくは数時間の違いであっても、彼らが伝えようとしている内容と矛盾する大統領からの宣告によってしばしば足をすくわれていた。

5 バイデンチームには、大統領本人と代弁者間の見解の一貫性、および、政策決定過程の尊重がある。バイデン氏の閣僚は、大統領が何を望んでいるか知っており、目的と手段の関係をきちんと理解しているから、組織から外れた行動を取ることはない。

6 新政権には2つの危険な要素がある。一つ目は自信過剰だ。この集団は自分たちの仕事を心得ている。何人かはほんの4年前に同様の地位に就いていた。しかしその後、世界は変貌しており、バイデンチームはその展開を把握して対応する必要がある。次期大統領は閣僚候補を発表する際、この新しい現実を認め、「このチームは比類のない経験と実績を備えている一方、旧態依然とした思考と代わり映えのない習慣ではこれらの難局に対応できないという考えも反映している」と説

明した。任務の中心になるのは、同盟国が機能し、運営される方法の変革である。

7 成功には、トランプ氏の「米国第一」政策の裏にあるポピュリズムが消えてはいないという認識が必須である。外交政策は中産階級の利益によりかなうものでなければならず、エリートの道具と見なされてはならない。国家安全保障担当補佐官のジェイク・サリバン氏はそのことをよく知っている。サリバン氏はこの問題に焦点を当てた対策委員会で働いていた。バイデン政権の政策を持続可能なものにするには、サリバン氏は、政権が間違いなくその知識を活かすよう努めなければならない。

8 その論理が行き着くのは、トランプ政権が採用してきた、国家安全保障についてのより広い（そして、おそらく適切な範囲を超えた）定義である。政策決定者は、経済の安定と国家安全保障の結び付きをよりうまく活用できるようにしなければならない。日本は、国家安全保障会議と国家安全保障局の再編を経て、その方向に移行しつつある。米国の場合、それは、大国間の競争が多次元にわたっている世界で、司法長官と財務長官、商務長官が肝要な役割を果たすことを意味する。

9 主な競争相手は中国であり、アジアにおいて（そして、次第に欧州においても）米国の同盟国は、中国の不正行為を終わらせ、中国政府の影響力の広がりを封じ込める努力に参加するよう求められるだろう。対中政策は、新政権の真剣さと信頼性の最も重要な試験の一つとなり、中国と関わる準備ができている問題は綿密に精査されるだろう。バイデン氏は、別の一連の懸案に関わる取引のために同盟国の国益を犠牲にしたり、損なったりすることはできない。

10 日本は特に、バイデン氏の長年の友人で国際気候特使に起用されたジョン・ケリー氏の役割に注目するだろう。気候変動は、バラク・オバマ政権第2期の国務長官を務めたときのケリー氏にとって特徴的な案件で、彼はトランプ氏が就任6カ月後に撤回した取り決めであるパリ気候協定の米国首席交渉官だった。気候変動は深刻な脅威であり、中国の参加なしには解決不能だが、その過程で日本の正当な権利を犠牲にすることはできない。北朝鮮、台湾、イランに対応する場合も同じことだ。

11 バイデン政権が直面する第二の危険は共和党に関するものである。共和党は、新型コロナウイルス感染症（COVID-19）の大流行やそれが引き起こした不況などの国家的課題を克服するために新大統領と協力するのか、それとも、そうした困難に対処する取り組みを損ない、政府を不自由な状態にして邪魔をするために終わりのない調査を始め、指名の承認を拒否して新政権を妨害しようとするのか。バイデン氏は、自分が中央から統治でき、共和党が彼に加わると信じているが、最

バイデン政権誕生で米国は正常復帰へ

近の経緯を見ると楽観の根拠はほとんどない。2024年の大統領選に出馬したいという強い願望を持つフロリダ州選出のマルコ・ルビオ上院議員は、バイデン氏の新チームについて、「履歴書は素晴らしい…米国の衰退につながる、上品で秩序だったつなぎ政権になるだろう」と判定したとき、懐疑的な態度が当然必要だと確証したが、「私たちを中国に依存させた『正常』に戻ることにはまったく興味がない」とも付け加えた。

12 米政府や日本政府にもそうした興味を持つ人はほとんどいない。課題は、政権を構築し、その政権を、平和的で繁栄した世界を維持するために米国と同盟国の資源を集結させるような、信頼が置けて一貫した政策を作る目的のために使うことだ。バイデン氏はよいスタートを切ったように見える。　　　　　（訳・注　中村）

第2章 国内政治・外交

9月14日、自民党総裁に選出され、拍手に応える菅官房長官（当時）

Tokyo's gubernatorial race holds lessons for the nation

日本全体にさまざまな教訓を投げ掛けた都知事選

July 9, 2020　　　　　　　　　　　●Tracks 31-36 / 訳 pp. 110-111

Track 31

1　Was it COVID-19 that worked favorably for the incumbent governor? Was it because the ruling Liberal Democratic Party didn't field a candidate? There could be many reasons why Tokyo Gov. Yuriko Koike won a second term in Sunday's election.

2　It was unfortunate that the lackluster campaign failed to garner much public attention despite Tokyo being the nation's capital. But the election result should not be easily dismissed as it has many implications for national politics. The lessons to be learned are not only for Tokyoites, but also for people nationwide.

Track 32

3　The impact of the novel coronavirus on the election was huge. Ms. Koike refrained from making stump speeches and avoided public appearances. Other candidates followed suit. Heated policy debate among the candidates was scarce during the campaign period as Ms. Koike was often absent from the events organized by media organizations. As a result, media coverage of the campaign was far less than in the last gubernatorial election, and there were not enough opportunities for voters to learn about the candidates and their policies.

4　In this election, campaigning mainly took place in cyberspace. Expectations may have been high that online campaigning could reach younger voters, but in reality online searches for election-related content appear to have been limited to those with a keen interest in politics.

▼ About This Editorial ▼

日本全体がコロナ禍に見舞われている最中に行われた今回の東京都知事選挙では、元自民党所属、都民ファーストの会・希望の党代表も務めた現職の小池百合子都知事が連日のメディア露出も追い風となって安定の勝利を収め、二期目を務めることになった。本来はコロナ対策だけでなく、さまざまな争点があったはずだが議論が白熱せず、事前の予想に近い結果となった。

1
- ☐ [タイトル]gubernatorial 知事の
- ☐ [タイトル]lesson 教訓、学ぶべき点
- ☐ favorably 有利に
- ☐ incumbent 現職の
- ☐ the Liberal Democratic Party 自由民主党、自民党
- ☐ ruling 与党である
- ☐ field 候補者を立てる
- ☐ candidate 候補者

2
- ☐ lackluster 精彩に欠ける
- ☐ campaign 選挙運動
- ☐ fail to *do* ～できない
- ☐ garner 獲得する
- ☐ capital 首都
- ☐ dismiss 簡単に片付ける
- ☐ implication 示唆、意味合い
- ☐ national politics 国政
- ☐ Tokyoite 東京都民
- ☐ nationwide 国全体の

3
- ☐ impact of A on B AのBへの（強い）影響
- ☐ novel 新種の、新型の
- ☐ huge 非常に大きな
- ☐ refrain from *doing* ～することを差し控える
- ☐ stump 遊説(の)
- ☐ public appearance 公衆の面前に姿を現すこと
- ☐ follow suit その例に倣う、追随する
- ☐ heated 熱の入った
- ☐ scarce ほとんどない
- ☐ absent from ... …に参加しない
- ☐ organize 企画[主催]する
- ☐ media メディア、マスコミ
- ☐ coverage 報道
- ☐ far はるかに、ずっと
- ☐ opportunity 機会
- ☐ voter 有権者

4
- ☐ take place 行われる
- ☐ cyberspace ネット上の空間、オンライン
- ☐ expectation(s) 期待
- ☐ reach 訴え掛ける、届く
- ☐ in reality 実際には、現実は
- ☐ those with ... …を持った人々
- ☐ keen 熱意ある、熱烈な

Track 33

5 Ms. Koike frequently posted messages on social media, such as Instagram and YouTube, but many of her YouTube videos only attracted several thousand views each. It's hard to say that she was successful in reaching a wider audience.

6 Since the pandemic is likely to continue for the coming months at least, candidates in subsequent elections will need to explore ways to deliver their policy messages without direct contact with voters and the media must step up their efforts to report on the campaigns and candidates' policy differences so people can be better informed.

Track 34

7 Voter turnout for the latest Tokyo race was 55 percent, down 4.73 percent from the previous election. Though the figure is still higher than most of the national elections in the past decade, nearly half the eligible voters in the nation's capital didn't cast ballots.

8 Political apathy clearly isn't a phenomenon limited to Tokyo. Voter turnout in Diet elections has been declining. It dropped from a high of 70 percent in the 2009 Lower House election—which saw the opposition Democratic Party of Japan take power—to 53.68 percent in the 2017 general election. Efforts must be made to engage voters in the political process before the next national election.

Track 35

9 The failure of the opposition parties to form a united front also contributed to Ms. Koike's sweeping victory—a lesson that applies to future national elections.

5
- □ post 投稿する、Web上に公開する
- □ social media ソーシャルメディア、SNS →英語ではSNSとは言わない
- □ attract 引き付ける
- □ view 閲覧
- □ audience （動画）視聴者

6
- □ pandemic パンデミック、（疫病の）世界的流行
- □ coming この先の
- □ subsequent 今後の
- □ explore 探求[模索]する
- □ deliver 伝える、届ける
- □ step up 強める
- □ report 報道する
- □ difference 違い
- □ so ... can *do* …が〜できるように
- □ be informed 情報を持っている、知らされている

7
- □ voter turnout 投票率→turnoutは「参加者数[率]」の意
- □ figure 数字
- □ national election 国政選挙
- □ the past decade 過去10年
- □ eligible 資格のある
- □ cast a ballot 票を投じる

8
- □ apathy 無関心
- □ phenomenon 現象
- □ Diet 国会（議員）の
- □ the Lower House 下院、（日本の）衆議院
- □ see （時代などが）…を目撃する
- □ the Democratic Party of Japan 民主党→2016年に維新の党と合流
- □ opposition 野党（の）、反対勢力（の）
- □ take power 政権を握る
- □ general election 総選挙
- □ engage A in B AをBに引き込む[参加させる]

9
- □ form a united front 統一戦線を結成する、一致団結する
- □ contribute to ... …に寄与する
- □ sweeping victory 圧勝
- □ apply 当てはまる

10   The main interest of Tokyo voters was how to overcome the crisis caused by the COVID-19 outbreak. According to an exit poll of 2,755 people by Asahi Shimbun, 64 percent responded favorably to Ms. Koike's coronavirus countermeasures, and of those, 75 percent voted for her. On the other hand, 34 percent did not approve of the steps she took. Of them, 27 percent voted for Kenji Utsunomiya, the former head of the Japan Federation of Bar Associations, and 17 percent cast ballots for Taisuke Ono, a former vice governor of Kumamoto Prefecture who was backed by Nippon Ishin no Kai. Ms. Koike clearly benefited from the divided opposition in addition to the advantage she enjoyed as the incumbent and the exposure she received from appearing on TV almost daily in recent months to give updates on the COVID-19 crisis.

Track 36

11   The Tokyo election campaign also failed to address many key problems that are equally important at the national level. For example, candidates expressed their opinions on the Tokyo Olympic and Paralympic Games, but didn't discuss remedies for issues such as the need for more childcare facilities, ballooning social security costs, or how to bolster Tokyo's once-ample reserve funds, which have been drained by the virus countermeasures taken over the past two months.

12   How to resuscitate the economy while protecting the public health is a matter that must be dealt with by political leaders on both the local and national level. Tokyo isn't the only place where the population is rapidly aging, either. Political leaders need to hammer out measures to tackle these pressing issues, and voters must realize that they have the power to change the course of Japan.

10
- □ overcome 乗り越える
- □ crisis 危機
- □ outbreak (疫病の)大流行
- □ exit poll (投票所)出口調査
- □ respond 反応を示す
- □ favorably 好意的に
- □ countermeasure(s) 対策
- □ vote for ... …に投票する
- □ approve of ... …を支持する
- □ step(s) 方策、対策
- □ former head 元会長
- □ the Japan Federation of Bar Associations 日本弁護士連合会
  → (the) barは「法曹界」
- □ vice governor 副知事
- □ back 後援する
- □ benefit from ... …の恩恵を受ける
- □ divided 分裂した
- □ in addition to ... …に加えて
- □ advantage 有利な点
- □ enjoy 享受する
- □ exposure 露出、メディアに(顔が)出ること
- □ update 最新情報

11
- □ address (問題に)取り組む
- □ at the national level 全国規模で
- □ remedy 解決策
- □ issue 問題
- □ facility 施設
- □ balloon 急増する
- □ social security 社会保障
- □ bolster 強化する
- □ once-ample かつては潤沢だった
  → ampleは「豊富な」の意
- □ reserve fund (非常用の)積立金、予備資金
- □ drain 枯渇させる
- □ over …にわたって

12
- □ resuscitate 生き返らせる、再生する
- □ public 国民の、市民の
- □ deal with a matter 問題に取り組む
- □ on both the local and national level 地方行政・国政両方のレベルで
- □ age 高齢化する
- □ hammer out 打ち出す
- □ measure(s) 方策、対策
- □ pressing 喫緊の、差し迫った
- □ course 針路、進むべき方向

Bump up the target for increasing renewable energy

再生可能エネルギー利用を増やす目標をさらに高めよ

August 17, 2020　　　　　　　●Tracks 37-41 / 訳 pp. 112-114

Track 37

1 Japan remains far behind many other advanced economies in the use of renewable energy such as wind and solar power. The government is now weighing a new set of measures to promote renewable energy, including expanding offshore wind power and reviewing the rules on access to the power transmission system— one of the key hurdles to increased use of renewables.

2 These efforts should be backed up by a much more aggressive target for increasing renewable energy in this country—to prompt greater investments in the sector and to drive home the government's commitment to de-carbonizing the nation's energy policy in the fight against climate change.

Track 38

3 The government's basic energy policy calls for turning renewables into a principal source of power supply. However, the target share for renewable energy in the 2030 power supply mix—22-24 percent of the total—is even lower than the 26 percent envisioned for coal-fired power plants, which many other industrialized nations plan to phase out because they emit more global warming gases such as carbon dioxide than other sources of power. Renewable energy including large-scale hydraulic power accounted for 17 percent of the nation's power supply in fiscal 2018—nearly double the 9 percent in 2010 but still well below the levels in advanced European economies.

▼ About This Editorial ▼

地球温暖化は世界の多くの国々が危機感を共有し、2020年以降の国際的な防止の枠組みに関しパリ協定が2015年に結ばれるも、2017年にトランプ米大統領が同協定からの脱退を表明するなど、世界の足並みがそろわない。日本も菅首相が所信表明演説で2050年までの温室効果ガス排出実質ゼロを打ち出したが、もっと対策を急ぐ必要はないのだろうか。

1
- □ [タイトル]bump up 高める
- □ [タイトル]renewable 再生可能な→第3段落では名詞で「再生可能エネルギー」の意
- □ far behind ... …に遠く及ばないで、大きく遅れて
- □ economy 経済体→経済単位としての国や地域
- □ weigh 検討する
- □ a set of ... 一連の…
- □ measure(s) 方策、施策
- □ offshore 沖合の
- □ access to ... …の利用権
- □ power transmission 送電
- □ hurdle 障害

2
- □ back up 支える
- □ aggressive 積極的な
- □ sector 業界、(産業)分野
- □ drive home 強調する
- □ commitment 関与、取り組み
- □ de-carbonizing 脱炭素化→二酸化炭素排出を抑えること
- □ climate change 気候変動

3
- □ call for ... …を求める
- □ turn A into B AをBに変える
- □ principal 主要な
- □ power supply 電力供給
- □ target share 目標割合
- □ mix 全体の配分、内訳→発電における水力・火力・原子力などの発電形態別の混合割合
- □ envision 構想[計画]する
- □ coal-fired 石炭火力の
- □ power plant 発電所
- □ industrialized nation 先進工業国
- □ phase out 段階的になくす
- □ emit 排出する
- □ global warming gas 地球温暖化ガス
- □ carbon dioxide 二酸化炭素
- □ hydraulic 水力の
- □ account for ... (数値・割合が)…を占める
- □ fiscal …会計年度
- □ well かなり、はるかに

4   When most of the nation's nuclear power plants were shut down following the 2011 meltdowns at Tokyo Electric Power Company Holdings' Fukushima No.1 nuclear power plant, the power industry fired up more thermal power plants, including coal, to make up for the loss of nuclear power, which supplied 30 percent of the nation's electricity demand before the disaster. Favored for its cheaper cost and the low geographical risk involved in its supply from overseas, the share of coal power reached 32 percent in 2018, second only to the 38 percent of natural gas-fired plants.

Track 39

5   In recent years, Japan has come under growing international fire for its heavy reliance on coal despite the global efforts to reduce carbon dioxide emissions. In response to such criticism, the government last month fleshed out its earlier pledge to phase out "inefficient" coal-fired power plants. Of the nation's 150 coal plants, 120 were categorized as less efficient in their power generation, and about 100 of them are expected to be set aside for either decommissioning or suspension from service by 2030.

6   However, the impact of the move on combating climate change may not be as big as the numbers suggest. Most of the coal plants to be put out of service are old, small-capacity facilities. The more "efficient" ones that will be kept, including those now planned or under construction, have much larger capacities so the net reduction in the total capacity of coal-fired plants in Japan will only amount to some 20 percent, according to an estimate by an environmental group.

4
- [ ] meltdown 融解
- [ ] Tokyo Electric Power Company Holdings 東京電力ホールディングス
- [ ] power industry 電力業界
- [ ] fire up（発電所を）始動する
- [ ] thermal 火力の
- [ ] make up for ... …を補う
- [ ] favor …のほうを好む
- [ ] for …が理由で
- [ ] geographical risk 地理的なリスク
- [ ] involved in ... …に関連する、…にまつわる
- [ ] second only to ... …に次いで2番目の
- [ ] natural gas 天然ガス

5
- [ ] come under fire 攻撃の的となる、批判を受ける
- [ ] growing 増大する
- [ ] reliance on ... …への依存
- [ ] emission 排出（量）
- [ ] in response to ... …に応えて
- [ ] flesh out 具体化する
- [ ] pledge 公約、約束
- [ ] of …の中で
- [ ] categorize A as B AをBに分類する
- [ ] power generation 発電
- [ ] set aside 除外する
- [ ] decommission（サービスを）廃止する、停止する
- [ ] suspension（一時）停止
- [ ] service 運用、使用

6
- [ ] combat 闘う
- [ ] put ... out of service …を稼働中止にする
- [ ] small-capacity 小出力の→capacity は「（発電）能力」の意
- [ ] be kept 保持される
- [ ] under construction 建設中の
- [ ] net 正味の、実質の、純…
- [ ] amount to ... （合計が）…に達する、及ぶ
- [ ] some（数字の前で）約…
- [ ] estimate 推計

Track 40

7　In fact, the government is not expected to change coal's share of 26 percent in the 2030 power supply mix. Even an "efficient" coal plant is said to emit twice as much carbon dioxide as a natural gas power plant, and many point to the global warming risk posed by keeping those plants in operation for decades to come.

8　Japan has pinned its hopes on nuclear energy—which does not emit carbon dioxide in generating power—for reducing its greenhouse gas emissions. However, the restart of nuclear plants idled in the wake of the 2011 Fukushima disaster remains slow. Nuclear power's share of electricity supply in 2018 was a mere 6 percent—a far cry from the government's target of 20-22 percent in 2030. Due to lingering safety concerns and the increased post-Fukushima cost of running nuclear plants, prospects are slim that the restart of the idled plants will pick up significant speed in the near future.

Track 41

9　Given the uncertain future of nuclear power and the nation's continued heavy dependence on fossil fuel-based energy, the government remains unable to upgrade its commitments to cut greenhouse gas emissions under the Paris Agreement to fight climate change—even though nations are urged to revamp their voluntary plans every five years to prevent the catastrophic effects of global warming. Significantly boosting the use of renewable energy holds the key to Japan accelerating its decarbonization efforts, and the government needs to make its commitment clear by sharply upgrading its targets for the share of renewables in energy supply.

7
- □ be expected to *do* ～すると考えられている
- □ coal's share 石炭火力発電が占める割合
- □ twice as much A as B Bの2倍の量のA
- □ many 多くの人々
- □ point to ... …を指摘する
- □ pose 引き起こす
- □ keep ... in operation …を稼働させ続ける
- □ ... to come この先…

8
- □ pin A on B A(希望など)をBにかける
- □ greenhouse gas 温室効果ガス→地球温暖化の元凶とされている
- □ restart 再稼働
- □ idle 稼働停止状態にする
- □ in the wake of ... …の余波を受けて
- □ mere ほんの
- □ a far cry from ... …には遠く及ばない
- □ lingering 根強く残る
- □ post-Fukushima 福島第一原発事故後の
- □ prospect 見通し
- □ slim ほんのわずかな
- □ pick up speed 加速する
- □ significant 著しい

9
- □ given …を考えると
- □ fossil fuel-based 化石燃料から生み出された→fossil fuelは石油・石炭・天然ガスなど
- □ upgrade 水準を上げる
- □ the Paris Agreement パリ協定→気候変動抑制に関する多国間の協定で、2015年採択
- □ be urged to *do* ～することが迫られている
- □ revamp 修正する、改訂する
- □ every …ごとに
- □ catastrophic 破滅的な
- □ boost 増大させる、高める
- □ hold the key to ... …(へ)の鍵を握っている
- □ accelerate 加速する
- □ decarbonization 脱炭素化

10 The higher cost of renewable energy in Japan compared to other countries where the use of those energy sources have become more prevalent, as well as the unstable power generation by renewable sources dependent on weather conditions, have often been cited as reasons why renewables don't take off in this country. Rather than continue to use those problems as excuses for dragging our feet, we must pursue technological innovations to overcome them and lower the cost of renewables. It's time to shift gears in the effort to restructure the nation's energy landscape.

10

- □ prevalent 普及した
- □ unstable 不安定な
- □ dependent on ... …次第の
- □ cite 挙げる
- □ take off 普及［成功］する
- □ excuse 言い訳
- □ drag *one's* feet 事をのろのろと進める、二の足を踏む

- □ pursue 目指す、追求する
- □ technological innovation 技術革新
- □ overcome 克服する
- □ lower 下げる
- □ shift gears 方針を変える
- □ restructure 再構築する
- □ landscape 様相、構図

Work-style reform needed at the government's center

政府中枢で求められる「働き方改革」

August 20, 2020　　　　　　　●Tracks 42-48 / 訳 pp. 115-117

Track 42

1 Earlier this month, a shocking survey result was announced. The survey, conducted by work-style consultancy Work-Life Balance Co. on 480 public servants between March and May, revealed that a distressing number of bureaucrats in government ministries have been logging overtime at a level that could cause death from overwork.

2 Due particularly to the spread of COVID-19, some 40 percent of the officials surveyed who work in the bureaucratic ground zero of Tokyo's Kasumigaseki district have been putting in a whopping 100 hours of overtime or more per month.

Track 43

3 Many workers at Japanese firms were once considered "corporate warriors" who spent more time in the office than at home. But now, the concept of work-life balance has gradually penetrated the private sector, and the recent pandemic has also forced businesses across a wide spectrum to accept telework and other flexible work styles. It is now time to review the work style of government employees to improve efficiency.

the japan times *alpha*

「The Japan Times Alpha」は
ジャパンタイムズが発行する英語
学習者のための週刊紙です。
その週に起きた重要なニュース、
世界中のトレンドなどの英文記事を
無理なく読み切れるボリュームで掲
載。和訳・解説付きなので、辞書
をひく手間を省いて効率的に英語表
現をインプットし、日本や世界の「今」
を語る英語力をつけるのに最適です。

● 毎週金曜日発行　● タブロイド判　24頁(標準)

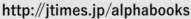

先の安倍政権が打ち出した「働き方改革」。2019年4月からは、働き方改革関連法案が順次施行され、「働く人々が、個々の事情に応じた多様で柔軟な働き方を自分で選択できるようにするための改革」(厚生労働省)が進むはずなのだが、足元の中央官庁では、変化を妨げる要因や旧態依然とした慣習が、官僚たちのより人間らしい生活の実現を阻み続けている。

1
- □ earlier this month 今月これまでに、今月に入って
- □ survey 調査
- □ conduct 実施する
- □ consultancy コンサルタント業者
- □ on …を対象として
- □ public servant 公務員
- □ distressing 悲惨な
- □ bureaucrat 官僚
- □ ministry 省、省庁
- □ log 記録を取る
- □ overtime 時間外労働

2
- □ due to ... …が原因で
- □ particularly 特に
- □ spread まん延
- □ some (数字の前で)約…
- □ bureaucratic 官庁[官僚]の
- □ ground zero 中心地
- □ put in (時間を)つぎ込む
- □ whopping 驚異的な

3
- □ firm 会社、企業
- □ corporate 企業(の)
- □ warrior 戦士
- □ concept 概念、考え方
- □ penetrate 浸透する
- □ private sector 民間企業
- □ pandemic パンデミック、(疫病の)世界的流行→COVID-19の世界的広がりを指す
- □ force ... to *do* …に〜することを余儀なくさせる
- □ business 会社、企業
- □ across a wide spectrum 広範囲にわたって
- □ review 見直す
- □ efficiency 効率

4   Environment Minister Shinjiro Koizumi, who announced the survey's results with Work-Life Balance's president, Yoshie Komuro, relayed one of the responses written by a health ministry official in his 30s: "My son told me that it was the first time for me to sit down with him and have dinner (on a weekday). I cried because I felt very sorry for my son that I hadn't done things that an ordinary parent would do. I realized the work style of Kasumigaseki is based on such sacrifice of the families of those bureaucrats."

`Track 44`

5   Because of the pandemic, the workload at government ministries and agencies has piled up, but because of the stay-home period it is also true that some bureaucrats have been able to spend more time with their families.

6   A major reason why government officials can't change their work style is that politicians refuse to adapt themselves to the digital age and continue to ask bureaucrats to give various briefings in person, even late at night or early in the morning. Fax messages and telephone calls continue to be their regular communication methods. Bureaucrats always have to promptly respond to requests from those lawmakers in such archaic ways.

`Track 45`

7   According to the survey, 80 percent of the respondents said briefings for politicians are conducted in person and not online, while 90 percent noted that they feel politicians don't have consideration for bureaucrats and their work environment.

8   Even though they should be urgently adopting a paperless system, 86 percent of the bureaucrats said they have to use faxes to send messages to politicians.

4
- environment minister 環境大臣
- relay (発言通りに)伝える
- health ministry 厚生労働省→正式英語名称は Ministry of Health, Labour and Welfare
- in one's 30s 30代の
- ... would do …であればするだろう →would に仮定の意味合いが含まれる
- sacrifice 犠牲

5
- workload 仕事量
- government agency 官庁
- pile up 積み上がる

6
- politician 政治家→ここでは国会議員を指す
- adapt oneself to ... …に順応する
- briefing (簡潔な)状況説明、ブリーフィング
- in person 直に会って、対面で
- promptly 迅速に
- respond to ... …に応じる
- lawmaker 国会議員
- archaic 時代遅れの

7
- respondent 回答者
- note コメントする
- consideration 思慮

8
- urgently 早急に
- adopt 採用する
- paperless 紙資料を使わない、デジタル化された

Track 46

9 While many politicians favor face-to-face communication, traditional methods of doing business are also deeply rooted in every sector of the government. For example, using documents and *hanko* seals are a main means for policy approval, while the use of online conference tools is limited, with some bureaucrats commenting that they can't use videoconferencing apps except Skype.

10 To change the government, digitalization of the Diet is also key. In mid-March, Hayato Suzuki, a Lower House member of the ruling Liberal Democratic Party, launched a project team with other young lawmakers. They are proposing that the Diet adopt online conference tools and enable lawmakers to vote remotely if they are unable to go to the Diet due to official duties, pregnancy or illness.

Track 47

11 After state minister of health Gaku Hashimoto and parliamentary vice minister Hanako Jimi went onboard the coronavirus-stricken cruise ship Diamond Princess in the port of Yokohama in February to inspect the ship, they were unable to go to the Diet for the quarantine period of two weeks. During this time there were deliberations on the national budget, but they were unable to participate.

12 Japan needs to create new rules and a system that fits the new age. In the future, an increase in female politicians would mean more will be giving birth when the Diet is in session, while more people with disabilities may also become Diet members. Ministers meanwhile may have to go overseas to conduct important official duties. Article 56 of the Constitution requires both houses of the Diet to have one-third or more members in attendance to hold a plenary session and vote, but if online voting without physically being present in the Diet can be done, this requirement can be met in the virtual realm.

9
- ☐ favor 好む
- ☐ face-to-face 対面での
- ☐ be deeply rooted in ... …に深く根付いている
- ☐ seal 印鑑
- ☐ means 手段
- ☐ approval 承認
- ☐ limited 限定的な
- ☐ videoconference ビデオ会議をする
- ☐ app アプリ、ソフトウエア

10
- ☐ the Diet 国会
- ☐ key 鍵となる、重要な
- ☐ (the) Lower House 衆議院
- ☐ the Liberal Democratic Party 自由民主党、自民党
- ☐ ruling 政権を握っている、与党である
- ☐ launch 立ち上げる、始める
- ☐ propose 提案する
- ☐ pregnancy 妊娠

11
- ☐ state minister 副大臣→state minister of health は厚生労働副大臣
- ☐ parliamentary vice minister (大臣) 政務官→副大臣とともに大臣を補佐する
- ☐ go onboard ... …に乗船する
- ☐ ...-stricken …に襲われた
- ☐ inspect 視察する
- ☐ quarantine 防疫隔離、検疫
- ☐ deliberation 審議
- ☐ national budget 国家予算

12
- ☐ increase in ... …の増加
- ☐ give birth 出産する
- ☐ in session 会期中で
- ☐ disability 障害
- ☐ official duty 公務
- ☐ Article 56 第56条
- ☐ the Constitution 憲法
- ☐ require ... to *do* …に〜するよう求める[規定する]
- ☐ both houses 両院(衆議院と参議院)とも
- ☐ one-third 3分の1
- ☐ in attendance 出席して
- ☐ plenary session 本会議
- ☐ physically 物理的に
- ☐ requirement 規定、要件
- ☐ meet (要件などを)満たす
- ☐ in the virtual realm 仮想空間の中[オンライン]で

Track 48

13 Replacing old rules and practices with new ones will not only help improve the working environment of bureaucrats, it will surely save time and expenses for many people, which will ultimately mean saving taxpayer money.

14 The world is facing tremendous challenges due to the pandemic and Japan needs to prepare for a possible twin outbreak of COVID-19 and influenza this fall and winter. Unless the current inefficiency in the government is addressed, it will be extremely difficult for Japan's policy-making center to deal swiftly and effectively with future crises.

13
- [ ] replace A with B AをBに置き換える
- [ ] practice 慣習
- [ ] not only ... …だけでなく
- [ ] expense 費用
- [ ] ultimately 最終的には
- [ ] taxpayer 納税者(の)

14
- [ ] tremendous 途方もない
- [ ] challenge 難問
- [ ] twin 二重の
- [ ] outbreak (疫病の)大流行
- [ ] inefficiency 非効率性
- [ ] address 取り組む、対処する
- [ ] deal with ... …を処理する、…に対処する
- [ ] swiftly 迅速に
- [ ] crisis 危機→crisesは複数形

Formidable challenges ahead as Suga era begins

菅政権発足、その先に待ち受ける難題

September 17, 2020   ●Tracks 49-53 / 訳 pp. 118-119

Track 49

1   Yoshihide Suga was elected the 99th prime minister of Japan on Wednesday, succeeding Shinzo Abe who was forced to step down unexpectedly because of ill health. Mr. Suga was picked to ensure stability and continuity in government and policy. That is a mixed mandate given the uncertainties that Japan faces and its lengthening list of internal and external challenges. Mr. Suga has proven to be a capable, hardworking politician throughout a long and successful career, one that many thought would end with his tenure as the longest-serving chief cabinet secretary in Japanese history (a longevity that matched that of Mr. Abe in the Prime Minister's Office). Maintaining a good work ethic is only part of his new job, however—he must also have the vision and creativity that are necessary to surmount the country's many challenges. Here, the verdict is less certain.

2   Mr. Suga's personal story is a remarkable tale. A self-made man, the son of an Akita strawberry farmer with no political connections, Mr. Suga supported himself as he attended night school at Hosei University. He served as secretary to an LDP politician and then became a local city assemblyman in Yokohama before moving to the national legislature. He was a member of the first Abe Cabinet, serving as minister of communications. Mr. Suga remained loyal to Mr. Abe after illness forced him from the prime minister's office

▼ About This Editorial ▼

菅義偉氏が、9月16日、第99代内閣総理大臣に任命された。新型コロナウイルス感染拡大防止や経済再生をはじめとするさまざまな難題に直面しているが、それらの問題の対処で結果を残すことが、国民の支持と自民党政権の安定確保につながるだろう。

1
- [タイトル]formidable 手ごわい
- [タイトル]era 時代
- be elected 選出される
- prime minister 内閣総理大臣
- succeed …の後を継ぐ
- be forced to *do* ～することを余儀なくされる
- step down 退陣する
- unexpectedly 突然に
- ill health 体調不良
- pick 選ぶ
- stability 安定
- continuity 継続
- mixed いろいろなものが混ざった
- mandate 任務、信任
- given …を考慮すると
- uncertainties 不安定要素
- lengthening 長くなる
- internal 内部の
- external 外部の
- prove to be ... …であることを証明する
- capable 有能な
- tenure 任期
- longest-serving 在任期間が最長の
- chief cabinet secretary 内閣官房長官
- longevity (長い)在任期間
- Prime Minister's Office 首相官邸
- work ethic 職業倫理
- surmount 乗り越える
- verdict 判決、裁定

2
- personal story 身の上話、生い立ち
- remarkable 注目に値する、異例の
- tale 話
- self-made man たたき上げの人
- political connections 政治的な人脈
- support *oneself* 自活する
- attend (学校などに)通う
- night school 夜間学校
- serve as ... …として働く
- secretary 秘書
- LDP 自由民主党(の)
- local city assemblyman 地方市議会議員
- national legislature 国会
- the first Abe Cabinet 第一次安倍内閣
- minister of communications 総務大臣→Minister of Internal Affairs and Communications のこと
- remain 引き続き…のままでいる
- loyal to ... …に忠実な
- illness 病気
- force A from B AをBから追いやる

in 2007; for that devotion he was rewarded with the job of chief cabinet secretary, the second most powerful person in government, when Mr. Abe returned as prime minister in 2012.

Track 50

3 Mr. Suga won the top spot for himself in a parliamentary vote this week in which he secured large majorities in both the Lower and Upper Houses. His ascension to the Prime Minister's Office was assured after he prevailed in the Liberal Democratic Party (LDP) presidential ballot on Monday—in a contest where he won another mandate after claiming 377 of 534 votes.

4 Mr. Suga's election victories were assured. After first denying that he had any interest in the top slot, he was drafted by LDP leaders as the person best suited to continue the Abe program. That intent is evident in Mr. Suga's administration. Eight of Mr. Abe's 20 Cabinet ministers kept their jobs in the administration unveiled Wednesday, and another seven either moved to new Cabinet posts or were reappointed to those they held in previous administrations. Kingmakers retained their positions: Taro Aso, head of the party's second largest faction, continues as deputy prime minister and finance minister and Toshihiro Nikai, head of his own faction, remains LDP secretary general. The selection of Mr. Abe's younger brother, Nobuo Kishi, as defense minister—his first Cabinet post—strengthens Mr. Suga's claim to his predecessor's support (if that was ever in doubt).

- ☐ devotion 献身
- ☐ be rewarded with ...（褒美として）…を与えられる
- ☐ second most powerful 二番目に力を持つ

3
- ☐ top spot 首位の座
- ☐ parliamentary vote 国会での投票
- ☐ secure 確保する
- ☐ large majority 大多数
- ☐ the Lower and Upper Houses 衆参両院
- ☐ ascension to ... …への昇進
- ☐ be assured 保証される
- ☐ prevail 勝つ
- ☐ presidential ballot 総裁選挙
- ☐ contest 闘い→ここでは選挙のこと
- ☐ claim 獲得する

4
- ☐ election 選挙
- ☐ victory 勝利
- ☐ deny 否定する
- ☐ interest 関心、意欲
- ☐ top slot トップの地位
- ☐ be drafted 選抜される
- ☐ best suited to *do* ～するのに最適の
- ☐ continue 継続する
- ☐ program 政治要綱、政策
- ☐ intent 意向
- ☐ be evident in ... …にはっきりと見てとれる
- ☐ administration 陣営、内閣
- ☐ keep *one's* job 職を維持する
- ☐ unveil 発表する
- ☐ be reappointed to ... …に再任される
- ☐ previous 前の
- ☐ kingmaker 政界権力者
- ☐ retain …を持ち続ける
- ☐ faction 派閥
- ☐ deputy prime minister 副総理
- ☐ finance minister 財務相
- ☐ secretary general 幹事長
- ☐ defense minister 防衛相
- ☐ Cabinet post 閣僚ポスト
- ☐ strengthen 強化する
- ☐ claim 主張
- ☐ predecessor 前任者
- ☐ in doubt 疑わしい

Track 51

5 He will need all the help he can get. Mr. Suga faces imposing challenges: Most of them would occupy any occupant of the Prime Minister's Office, but some are his alone. The immediate concerns are obvious: keeping the COVID-19 outbreak under control and getting the economy, which is suffering a historical contraction, back on track. The postponed 2020 Olympic and Paralympic Games are another priority. Mr. Suga said that he wants to promote deregulation and structural reform, the so-called "third arrow" in the Abenomics quiver and the one that is believed to have never truly taken flight.

6 On foreign policy, he must keep strong the relationship with the United States—a tricky assignment given the special relationship that Mr. Abe had with U.S. President Donald Trump—while stabilizing and advancing relations with China. Both are difficult given tensions between Washington and Beijing and the extraordinary churn in geopolitics, but they are even more of a challenge for Mr. Suga, whose foreign policy experience is limited. A comparison with Mr. Abe's efforts—and unquestioned successes—in this arena will shine an even brighter light on his successor's shortcomings.

Track 52

7 Mr. Suga's career has been marked by hard work and pragmatism. He knows how to maneuver in and among the bureaucracy. But those efforts have been in the service of someone else's agenda. This is his potentially biggest weakness. Mr. Suga has no support base of his own and he never joined a faction. It is easier to push initiatives as a member of the LDP's biggest faction, as Mr. Abe was, or when he has the public behind him, as Junichiro Koizumi did. The effort to highlight Mr. Suga's connection to the people

5
- □ imposing 威圧的な、圧倒されるような
- □ occupy 多忙な状態にする
- □ occupant 在任者
- □ immediate 当面の
- □ concern 懸案事項
- □ obvious 明らかな
- □ keep ... under control …を抑制する
- □ COVID-19 新型コロナウイルス感染症→Coronavirus Disease 2019の略
- □ outbreak (疫病の) 大流行
- □ get ... back on track …を再び軌道に乗せる
- □ suffer 苦しむ
- □ historical 歴史的な
- □ contraction 縮小、後退
- □ postponed 延期された
- □ priority 優先事項
- □ promote 推進する
- □ deregulation 規制緩和
- □ structural reform 構造改革
- □ so-called いわゆる
- □ third arrow 第三の矢
- □ quiver 矢筒
- □ take flight 飛び立つ

6
- □ foreign policy 外交政策
- □ tricky やりにくい
- □ assignment 任務、役目
- □ stabilize 安定させる
- □ advance 前進させる
- □ tension 緊張
- □ extraordinary 途方もない
- □ churn 混乱
- □ geopolitics 地政学
- □ more of a ... 一層の…である
- □ experience 経験
- □ limited 限られた
- □ comparison 比較
- □ effort(s) 取り組み、努力
- □ unquestioned 疑う余地のない
- □ arena 活躍の舞台
- □ shine a light on ... …に光を当てる
- □ successor 後任
- □ shortcoming(s) 弱み

7
- □ be marked by ... …を特徴とする
- □ pragmatism 現実主義
- □ maneuver うまく立ち回る
- □ in and among ... …内および…間で
- □ bureaucracy 官僚社会、官僚たち
- □ in the service of ... …に仕える、…に役立つ
- □ agenda 課題、政策
- □ potentially 潜在的に
- □ weakness 弱点
- □ support base 支持基盤
- □ push 推進する
- □ initiative 新たな取り組み
- □ have A behind B AをBの後ろ盾とする
- □ the public 国民
- □ highlight …を強調する

since he declared his candidacy has only underscored how much work has to be done on this front.

8 Mr. Suga's reported preference for solving problems that impact ordinary citizens—reducing phone bills, increasing day care centers or promoting tourism—should help him make that all-important connection to the public. Addressing those concerns will go a long way to meeting his most important job requirement: ensuring an LDP victory in the next general election. Mr. Abe led his party to six consecutive national election triumphs.

Track 53

9 Mr. Suga says he is focused on the COVID-19 crisis and the economy, and isn't thinking about ballots. Those are good priorities. Dealing with them successfully will win the public support that will power his party to election victory. It is a tough assignment that will demand skill, hard work and a fair bit of luck. Mr. Abe had all three—Mr. Suga must hope that he does, too.

☐ declare 表明する   ☐ underscore 明確に示す
☐ candidacy 立候補   ☐ front 領域

8
☐ reported 報じられている   ☐ tourism 観光
☐ preference 好み   ☐ all-important 極めて重要な
☐ solve a problem 問題を解決する   ☐ address a concern 問題に取り組む
☐ impact 影響を及ぼす   ☐ go a long way 大いに役に立つ
☐ ordinary citizens 一般市民   ☐ job requirement 職務要件
☐ reduce 減らす   ☐ general election 国政選挙
☐ phone bills 電話代   ☐ consecutive 連続の
☐ day care center 保育所   ☐ triumph 勝利

9
☐ be focused on ... …に集中している   ☐ tough 厳しい、大変な
☐ crisis 危機   ☐ demand 必要とする
☐ ballot 投票   ☐ skill 手腕
☐ deal with ... …に対処する   ☐ a fair bit of ... かなりの…
☐ win support 支持を得る   ☐ luck 運
☐ power 勢いづける

The 'Quad' offers hope for a Free and Open Indo-Pacific

日米豪印の「自由で開かれたインド太平洋」戦略に期待

October 8, 2020   ●Tracks 54-59 / 訳 pp. 120-122

Track 54

1　As foreign ministers from the Quadrilateral countries—Japan, the United States, Australia and India—met in Tokyo this week, speculation soared about the purpose of the group. It is alternatively a gathering of concerned countries to contain a revisionist China, a forum to promote a Free and Open Indo-Pacific region and even the cornerstone of a nascent regional security architecture. The "Quad" (as it is called) can be all those things but its future is uncertain, and its eventual form and content depend on how it is managed.

2　The Quadrilateral Security Dialogue was launched in 2007 during Prime Minister Shinzo Abe's first term in office. It collapsed the following year when Australia withdrew amidst criticism from Chinese officials that the group was an anti-China bloc and as doubts grew over whether the participants shared aims and objectives.

Track 55

3　Mounting concern about Chinese behavior prompted the four countries to try again. They resurrected the Quad in 2017 and it has met at various levels ever since. This week's meeting was the second ministerial get-together; the first was last year in New York.

▼ About This Editorial ▼

日米豪印外相が10月6日、東京で会談し、「自由で開かれたインド太平洋」を推進する方針で一致した。勢力を拡大する中国に対抗する非公式な枠組みではあるが、参加国の関係を強化し他国に連携を広げることで、地域の安定に寄与することが期待される。

1
- ☐ [タイトル]Quad 日米豪印戦略対話、4カ国戦略対話→Quadrilateral Security Dialogueの略。quadrilateralは「4国間」の意
- ☐ [タイトル]Free and Open Indo-Pacific「自由で開かれたインド太平洋」→Indo-Pacificは「インド太平洋地域」の意
- ☐ foreign minister 外相
- ☐ speculation 憶測
- ☐ soar 膨らむ
- ☐ alternatively A, B and C Aであり、Bであり、Cでもある
- ☐ gathering 集会
- ☐ contain 封じ込める
- ☐ revisionist 修正主義の
- ☐ cornerstone 礎
- ☐ nascent 新生の
- ☐ security 安全保障
- ☐ architecture 構造
- ☐ eventual 最終的な

2
- ☐ launch 発足する
- ☐ term 任期
- ☐ in office 在任して
- ☐ collapse 失敗する
- ☐ following 次の
- ☐ withdraw 脱退する
- ☐ amidst …の中で
- ☐ criticism 批判
- ☐ bloc （国家間の）圏、連合
- ☐ doubt 疑念
- ☐ participant 参加国
- ☐ aim 目標
- ☐ objective 目的

3
- ☐ mounting 高まる
- ☐ concern 懸念
- ☐ behavior 行動
- ☐ prompt 駆り立てる
- ☐ resurrect 復活させる
- ☐ various さまざまな
- ☐ ever since それ以来
- ☐ ministerial 閣僚の
- ☐ get-together 集まり

87

4   While all four governments are troubled by Chinese behavior, the United States has been the loudest critic. U.S. Secretary of State Mike Pompeo spoke for his administration when he condemned China's "exploitation, corruption and coercion," and characterized its actions as "bullying." Japanese security planners agree, although they are unlikely to use such blunt language. China poses a territorial threat given the dispute over the Senkaku Islands and it is widely viewed as a revisionist power that seeks regional preeminence, which will come at a significant cost to Japan.

Track 56

5   Meanwhile, Australia objects to Chinese island building in the South China Sea (as do the others), interference in its domestic politics and the sanctions imposed on exports to China after Canberra complained about that interference and called for an international investigation into the origins of the COVID-19 outbreak. India has had decades of troubled relations with its neighbor to the north, culminating in armed clashes along their disputed border in the Himalayas a few weeks ago that led to the deaths of dozens of troops.

6   While attention has focused on military exercises that underscore the Quad members' aim to give their cooperation teeth, discussions are much more extensive, encompassing—among other topics— infrastructure, telecommunications systems (5G in particular), cybersecurity, intellectual property protections and responses to the COVID-19 outbreak. After this week's meetings, Japanese Foreign Minister Toshimitsu Motegi said the Quad members agreed to meet regularly, discuss views of and cooperate on those issues and others. He also reportedly proposed that the Quad broaden its cooperation with other countries.

4
- □ loud 声高に主張する
- □ critic 批判者
- □ Secretary of State 国務長官
- □ administration 政権
- □ condemn 非難する
- □ exploitation 搾取
- □ corruption 腐敗
- □ coercion 抑圧
- □ characterize A as B AをBであると見なす
- □ bullying いじめ
- □ blunt 露骨な
- □ pose a threat 脅威をもたらす
- □ territorial 領土の
- □ given …を考慮すると
- □ dispute over ... …をめぐる争い
- □ Senkaku Islands 尖閣諸島
- □ widely viewed as ... 広く…と見なされて
- □ seek 得ようとする
- □ preeminence 優位性
- □ come at a cost （費用が）高くつく

5
- □ meanwhile その一方で
- □ object to ... …に異議を唱える
- □ the South China Sea 南シナ海
- □ interference 干渉
- □ domestic politics 内政
- □ sanction(s) 制裁措置
- □ impose 課す
- □ Canberra オーストラリア政府
- □ call for ... …を求める
- □ investigation 調査
- □ origin 発生源
- □ COVID-19 新型コロナウイルス感染症→Coronavirus Disease 2019の略
- □ outbreak 大流行
- □ decades of ... 数十年に及ぶ…
- □ neighbor 隣国→中国のこと
- □ culminate in ... 結果的に…になる
- □ armed clash 武力衝突
- □ disputed 紛争中の
- □ the Himalayas ヒマラヤ山脈
- □ troop 兵士

6
- □ attention 注目
- □ focus on ... …に集中する
- □ military exercise 軍事演習→海上共同演習マラバールのこと。オーストラリアの参加は2007年以来
- □ underscore 明確に示す
- □ give ... teeth …を強化する
- □ cooperation 連携、協力
- □ extensive 広範囲に及ぶ
- □ encompass 網羅する
- □ telecommunications 電気通信
- □ in particular 特に
- □ intellectual property 知的財産
- □ protection 保護
- □ response 対応
- □ regularly 定期的に
- □ view 意見
- □ issue 問題
- □ reportedly 報じられるところによれば
- □ propose 提案する
- □ broaden 拡大する

Track 57

7 Expanding both the agenda and membership is a good idea, but it is still a long way from Mr. Pompeo's suggestion earlier in the week that the group be "institutionalized" and then "build out to a true security framework," with other countries joining "at the appropriate time."

8 That won't be for a while. Strategic coordination is one thing; a formal security mechanism is another. Japan has significantly strengthened security ties with Australia and India, but it faces legal constraints in making security commitments to other countries. All three countries—Japan, Australia and India—have issues with China but they also want to calibrate relations in ways that account for their geographic, economic and political realities. India's refusal to join the Regional Comprehensive Economic Partnership trade deal is a reminder of Delhi's reluctance to tie its hands in any formal way.

Track 58

9 China will make it even harder. Chinese Foreign Ministry spokesman Wang Wenbin warned against "forming exclusive cliques" and "targeting third parties or undermining third parties' interests," and called for "open, inclusive and transparent" cooperation that is "conducive to mutual understanding and trust between regional countries." Mr. Wang dismissed Mr. Pompeo's plans to form a coalition as "nonsense," adding "He won't see that day. And his successors won't see that day either, because that day will never, ever come."

7
- [ ] expand 拡大する
- [ ] agenda 議題
- [ ] membership 加盟国数
- [ ] be a long way from ... …には程遠い
- [ ] suggestion 提案
- [ ] institutionalize 制度化する
- [ ] build out 構築する
- [ ] framework 枠組み
- [ ] appropriate 適切な

8
- [ ] for a while しばらくの間
- [ ] strategic 戦略的
- [ ] coordination 連携
- [ ] A is one thing; B is another. AとBはまったくの別物である
- [ ] mechanism 枠組み
- [ ] significantly 大幅に
- [ ] security ties 安全保障関係
- [ ] face 直面する
- [ ] legal constraints 法的制約
- [ ] commitment 関与
- [ ] calibrate 調整する
- [ ] account for ... …を考慮する
- [ ] geographic 地理的な
- [ ] realities 実状
- [ ] refusal 拒否
- [ ] the Regional Comprehensive Economic Partnership 地域的な包括的経済連携、RCEP
- [ ] trade deal 貿易協定
- [ ] reminder 思い起こさせるもの
- [ ] Delhi インド政府
- [ ] reluctance to *do* 〜したがらないこと
- [ ] tie *one's* hands 自身の自由を束縛する

9
- [ ] foreign ministry 外務省、(中国の)外交部
- [ ] spokesman 報道官
- [ ] warn against ... …をけん制する
- [ ] form 組む
- [ ] exclusive 排他的な
- [ ] clique 徒党
- [ ] target 標的にする
- [ ] third party 第三者
- [ ] undermine 損ねる
- [ ] interest(s) 利益、利害
- [ ] inclusive 包括的な
- [ ] transparent 透明性のある
- [ ] conducive to ... …に資する
- [ ] mutual understanding 相互理解
- [ ] dismiss A as B AをBだとしてはねつける
- [ ] coalition 同盟、連合
- [ ] nonsense たわごと
- [ ] see that day その日を迎える
- [ ] successor 後継者

10 He may be right. China's behavior remains worrying, however. The Quad nations, along with other regional governments, know that their best chance of moderating Beijing's behavior is if they act together and speak in one voice. That does not mean that they must adopt identical policies: There is room for nuance and variegation as long as member governments are working toward the same goals and understand each other's objectives and tactics.

Track 59

11 Institutionalized cooperation serves another purpose: It forces the U.S. to engage in the region too. The Quad provides a window on U.S. decision-making and offers partner governments the opportunity to influence Washington's thinking on issues that are of vital concern to them.

12 While we share a commitment to a Free and Open Indo-Pacific region, that concept remains elastic and our national commitments to realize that vision remain a work in progress. The only way to make it real is through steady and ongoing communication, cooperation and coordination. The Quad is a vital mechanism to do just that—whatever form it takes.

10
- □ remain …のままである
- □ worrying 心配な
- □ nation 国
- □ along with ... …とともに
- □ (the) best chance of *doing* ～するための一番の方法
- □ moderate 抑制する
- □ Beijing 中国政府
- □ mean 意味する
- □ adopt 採用する
- □ identical まったく同じ
- □ room for ... …の余地
- □ nuance 微妙な差異
- □ variegation 多様(性)
- □ as long as ... …である限りは
- □ tactic(s) 戦略

11
- □ serve a purpose 目的にかなう、役立つ
- □ force ... to *do* …に(強制的に)～させる
- □ engage A in B AをBに関わらせる
- □ window 知る機会
- □ decision-making 意思決定
- □ offer 提供する
- □ influence 影響を及ぼす
- □ Washington 米国政府
- □ vital 極めて重要な

12
- □ share 共有する
- □ elastic 融通性のある
- □ realize 実現させる
- □ vision 構想
- □ work in progress 進行中の作業
- □ make ... real …を現実のものにする
- □ steady 地道な
- □ ongoing 継続的な
- □ whatever いかなる…であれ

Sticking with tradition, Mr. Suga makes Southeast Asia his priority

菅首相、伝統を守って東南アジアを最優先に

October 22, 2020　　　　●Tracks 60-66 / 訳 pp. 123-125

Track 60

1　Visiting the Southeast Asia nations of Vietnam and Indonesia this week on his first foreign trip since becoming prime minister, Yoshihide Suga was applauded for continuing the foreign policy program of his predecessor, Shinzo Abe. When Mr. Abe returned to power in 2012, he not only made Vietnam his first overseas stop but he visited all 10 members of the Association of Southeast Asian Nations (ASEAN) during his first year in office.

2　China is credited for making the region a priority for Tokyo, but Southeast Asia has always been one of Japan's vital interests. This country's leaders have long recognized that they need support from and friendly relations with their counterparts in the region. Those relationships have assumed greater value as Beijing becomes a more formidable diplomatic and economic partner and a security concern.

Track 61

3　The two-country, four-day trip was a success, an important achievement for a prime minister widely considered inexperienced in foreign affairs. Mr. Suga employed a simple formula: Get tangible deliverables on economic and security concerns. That focus makes sense given restrictions on diplomacy resulting from the COVID-19 outbreak. Large events were discouraged, reducing opportunities for people-to-people and cultural programming.

▼ About This Editorial ▼

外交を不安視されていた菅首相だが、初の外遊となったベトナム・インドネシア歴訪では成果を残した。中国の影響力がますます大きくなる中で、日本が東南アジア諸国との友好的な関係を維持しつつ、その存在感を発揮できるか、今後のかじ取りが注目される。

1
- □ [タイトル]stick with ... …を守り続ける
- □ [タイトル]tradition 伝統
- □ [タイトル]priority 最優先（事項）
- □ foreign trip 外国訪問、外遊
- □ prime minister 首相
- □ applaud 称賛する
- □ continue 継続する
- □ foreign policy 外交政策
- □ predecessor 前任者
- □ return to power 政権に復帰する
- □ overseas 外国の、海外の
- □ member 加盟国
- □ the Association of Southeast Asian Nations 東南アジア諸国連合、ASEAN
- □ in office 在任して

2
- □ be credited for ... …の原因である
- □ region 地域→ここではSoutheast Asia（東南アジア）を指す
- □ vital 極めて重要な
- □ interest(s) 利害関係
- □ recognize 認識する
- □ relation 関係
- □ counterpart 相当する人→ leader（首脳）を指す
- □ relationship 結び付き
- □ assume 帯びる
- □ formidable 手ごわい
- □ diplomatic 外交的な
- □ security 安全保障
- □ concern 懸念

3
- □ achievement 成果
- □ (be) widely considered ... …と広く見なされる
- □ inexperienced 経験のない
- □ foreign affairs 外交問題
- □ employ （手段などを）採用する
- □ formula 方式
- □ tangible 実体のある、具体的な
- □ deliverable 結果、成果
- □ given …を考慮すると
- □ restriction 制限
- □ diplomacy 外交
- □ result from ... …に由来する
- □ COVID-19 新型コロナウイルス感染症
- □ outbreak （疫病の）大流行
- □ discourage やめさせる
- □ opportunity 機会
- □ people-to-people 人と人の

4 On the economic front, Mr. Suga reportedly procured agreements in both countries to resume business travel between them and Japan, a priority as countries struggle to recover from the pandemic. Details remain to be worked out, but the need to facilitate business travel should provide the motivation needed to conclude arrangements.

Track 62

5 Mr. Suga's call for the diversification of supply chains was also well received. Japan, like other developed economies, is concerned about its reliance on China to fill critical nodes in its manufacturing processes. Tokyo has created funding mechanisms to help Japanese companies relocate some operations back to Japan or more widely throughout Southeast Asia. (The former has received attention; the latter has not.) Governments in Hanoi and Jakarta welcome increased investments in their country by Japanese companies.

6 That drive also spurred Mr. Suga to promise Indonesian President Joko Widodo that Japan would continue infrastructure projects, especially on high-speed trains, programs that make the country a more inviting site for private investment. Japan also announced that it would provide Indonesia a ¥50 billion ($470 million) loan for disaster prevention and to fight COVID-19.

Track 63

7 Just as important were security agreements. In Hanoi, Mr. Suga and Prime Minister Nguyen Xuan Phuc agreed to transfer Japanese defense technology and equipment to Vietnam; in that, too, specifics are to be worked out. That agreement follows a July deal between Vietnam and the Japan International Cooperation Agency (JICA) by which Hanoi will borrow ¥36.63 billion to build six coast guard patrol vessels, to be delivered by October 2025.

4
- [ ] front 面
- [ ] reportedly 伝えられるところでは
- [ ] procure 手に入れる
- [ ] resume 再開する
- [ ] business travel 業務渡航
- [ ] struggle 奮闘する
- [ ] recover 回復する
- [ ] pandemic パンデミック、(疫病の)世界的大流行
- [ ] detail(s) 詳細事項
- [ ] remain to *do* まだ〜していない
- [ ] work out 解決する
- [ ] facilitate 促進する
- [ ] motivation 動機
- [ ] conclude (取り決めなどを)成立させる
- [ ] arrangement 取り決め

5
- [ ] diversification 多様化
- [ ] supply chain サプライチェーン
- [ ] developed economy 先進国→この economy は「経済面から見た国」の意
- [ ] be concerned about ... …について心配する
- [ ] reliance 依存
- [ ] critical 重要な
- [ ] node 結び目
- [ ] manufacturing process 製造工程
- [ ] funding 資金調達(の)
- [ ] mechanism 仕組み
- [ ] relocate 移転させる
- [ ] operation 業務
- [ ] the former 前者
- [ ] the latter 後者
- [ ] investment 投資

6
- [ ] drive 流れ、傾向
- [ ] spur ... to *do* …に〜するよう促す
- [ ] infrastructure インフラ
- [ ] high-speed train 高速列車
- [ ] inviting 魅力的な
- [ ] private 民間の
- [ ] announce 発表する
- [ ] billion 10億
- [ ] loan 貸し付け
- [ ] disaster prevention 防災

7
- [ ] just as ... 同じように…である→この文では主語と補語が倒置されている
- [ ] transfer 移す
- [ ] defense technology 防衛技術
- [ ] equipment 装備品
- [ ] specifics 詳細
- [ ] deal 契約
- [ ] Japan International Cooperation Agency 国際協力機構(JICA)
- [ ] coast guard 沿岸警備隊
- [ ] patrol vessel 巡視艇
- [ ] deliver 引き渡す

8   In Jakarta, Mr. Suga and Mr. Widodo pledged to strengthen and deepen security and defense ties. Building on a 2015 agreement to enhance security cooperation in the South China Sea, they said they would hold a meeting of foreign and defense ministers at an early date and speed up talks on sales of defense-related equipment and technology.

Track 64

9   It is easy to see China as the force animating Mr. Suga's trip. Kunihiko Miyake, a former diplomat and now an advisor to the prime minister, explained in a Japan Times column earlier this week that China was "the elephant in the room" in meetings even if no one wanted to call it out by name. In remarks, Mr. Suga denounced moves "that go against the rule of law" in the South China Sea while emphasizing that "ASEAN and Japan fully share fundamental principles." He and Prime Minister Phuc agreed to cooperate on the Free and Open Indo-Pacific initiative.

10   That agreement is less than it seems. Cooperation is not endorsing, and that difference defines the gap between Japan and ASEAN governments, which insist that they are not on board with the vision. Instead, the Southeast Asian organization has developed the ASEAN Outlook on the Indo-Pacific, accepting the idea of an Indo-Pacific region but scrupulously avoiding endorsing a particular strategy. Mr. Suga tried to close the circle between Japan's vision and the ASEAN outlook by saying that he "strongly supports" a document that "powerfully sets forth the rule of law, openness, freedom, transparency and inclusiveness as ASEAN's principles for behavior."

8
- ☐ pledge 誓う、固く約束する
- ☐ strengthen 強化する
- ☐ deepen 深める
- ☐ tie(s) 関係
- ☐ build on ... …に基づく
- ☐ enhance 増強する
- ☐ the South China Sea 南シナ海
- ☐ minister 大臣
- ☐ at an early date 早い時期に
- ☐ speed up ... …を急ぐ、促進する
- ☐ defense-related 防衛関連の

9
- ☐ animate 突き動かす
- ☐ diplomat 外交官
- ☐ advisor to the prime minister 内閣官房参与
- ☐ explain 説明する
- ☐ the elephant in the room 部屋の中のゾウ→そこにいる誰もが認識しているが、触れないようにしている問題という意味
- ☐ even if ... たとえ…だとしても
- ☐ call ... out by name …を大声で名指しする
- ☐ remark 発言
- ☐ denounce 非難する
- ☐ the rule of law 法の支配
- ☐ emphasize 強調する
- ☐ fundamental 基本的な
- ☐ principle 原則
- ☐ cooperate 協力する
- ☐ the Free and Open Indo-Pacific initiative 「自由で開かれたインド太平洋」戦略

10
- ☐ endorse 承認する、賛成する
- ☐ difference 違い
- ☐ define 明示する、はっきり示す
- ☐ insist 主張する
- ☐ be on board with ... …に参加する
- ☐ vision ビジョン、未来像
- ☐ the ASEAN Outlook on the Indo-Pacific ASEANのインド太平洋構想
- ☐ accept 受け入れる
- ☐ scrupulously 用心深く
- ☐ avoid 避ける
- ☐ particular 特定の
- ☐ strategy 戦略
- ☐ close the circle 輪を閉じる、差を埋める
- ☐ set forth ... …を明らかにする、打ち出す
- ☐ openness 開放性
- ☐ transparency 透明性
- ☐ inclusiveness 包摂性
- ☐ behavior 行動

Track 65

11 Consistent with the principle of inclusivity—and seeking to defuse concerns in ASEAN capitals and silence complaints in Beijing—Mr. Suga denied that the Quad, the informal grouping of Japan, the United States, Australia and India that met earlier this month in Tokyo, had any intention of becoming an Asian version of NATO, the trans-Atlantic security organization. Rather, Japan and its partners "are willing to cooperate with any country that shares our thinking."

12 ASEAN governments' reluctance to anger Beijing stems from the outsize role China plays in their economies. It is the leading source of imports for all ASEAN members (save Brunei) and China's share of ASEAN total trade has swelled from 11.6% in 2009 to 18% in 2019. Those governments are wary of Beijing's readiness to use that trade as leverage or as a way to punish them for decisions with which it disagrees. Japanese trade, investment, aid and assistance is an attractive counterweight—and hedge against Chinese revisionism.

Track 66

13 Seeing those relationships through the prism of competition with China is a mistake, however. Mr. Suga was right to emphasize that Japan and ASEAN are "old friends" and that friendship is the real foundation for enduring and stable relations between them. Mr. Suga and his team must ensure that rhetoric is realized in practice and policy.

11
- ☐ (be) consistent with ... …と一貫している
- ☐ inclusivity 包摂性
- ☐ seek to *do* 〜しようとする
- ☐ defuse 和らげる
- ☐ capital 首都→ここではASEAN各国政府のこと
- ☐ silence 静かにさせる
- ☐ complaint 不満、苦情
- ☐ deny 否定する
- ☐ the Quad クアッド→Quadrilateral Security Dialogue（4カ国戦略対話）の通称
- ☐ informal 非公式な
- ☐ intention 意図
- ☐ NATO 北大西洋条約機構
- ☐ trans-Atlantic 大西洋の両側の
- ☐ be willing to *do* 〜する用意がある

12
- ☐ reluctance 気が進まないこと
- ☐ anger 怒らせる
- ☐ stem from ... …から生じる
- ☐ outsize 並外れて大きな
- ☐ save …を除いて→この save は前置詞
- ☐ swell 増大する
- ☐ be wary of ... …を警戒している
- ☐ readiness 準備ができていること
- ☐ leverage 影響力→「てこの作用」が本来の意味
- ☐ as a way to *do* 〜するための方法として
- ☐ punish 罰する
- ☐ disagree 意見を異にする
- ☐ attractive 魅力的な
- ☐ counterweight 対抗する力
- ☐ hedge against ... …に対する防止策、防衛手段
- ☐ revisionism 修正主義

13
- ☐ through the prism of ... …の視点で、…を通して
- ☐ competition 競争
- ☐ foundation 基盤
- ☐ enduring 永続的な
- ☐ stable 安定した
- ☐ ensure 確実にする
- ☐ rhetoric 言葉遣い、発言
- ☐ practice 実践

Following the crowd, Mr. Suga makes a bold climate pledge

気候問題で菅氏が他国に倣って大胆な公約

October 29, 2020 　　　　　　●Tracks 67-72 / 訳 pp. 126-128

Track 67

1　In his first policy speech to the Diet since taking office last month, Prime Minister Yoshihide Suga pledged to achieve zero emissions of greenhouse gases and realize a carbon-neutral society by 2050. It's a bold commitment, a stark contrast to his image as a staid and cautious politician. Achieving that goal will not be easy, but the objective is both smart and realizable.

2　Mr. Suga's speech has been applauded, but he was only aligning Japan with 120 other countries that have said that they too would achieve net-zero carbon dioxide emissions by 2050. His predecessor, Shinzo Abe, promised to reduce greenhouse gas emissions by 80% and reach carbon neutrality in the second half of this century. Mr. Suga was reportedly pushed to do more by Hiroshi Kajiyama, minister of economy, trade and industry, and Shinjiro Koizumi, the environment minister—the outward faces of Japan's energy and environmental policies—both of whom know well the diplomatic cost of their government's failure to lean forward on this issue.

所信表明演説で菅首相は、2050 年までに温室効果ガスの排出をゼロにし、脱炭素社会を実現すると公約した。これは、ほかの国々の方針に日本の歩調を合わせたもので、長年の石炭火力発電の政策を抜本的に転換し、再生可能エネルギーなどの利用によって、安定的電力供給を目指す。

1
- ☐ [タイトル]follow the crowd 多数派に従う
- ☐ [タイトル]pledge 公約
- ☐ policy speech 所信表明演説
- ☐ take office (政府の)役職に就く
- ☐ zero emission 排出ゼロ、ゼロエミッション→大気汚染物質や温室効果ガスの排出を実質ゼロにする仕組み
- ☐ greenhouse gas 温室効果ガス
- ☐ carbon-neutral society 脱炭素社会 →二酸化炭素の排出と吸収がプラスマイナスゼロの社会
- ☐ commitment 公約、深い関与
- ☐ stark まったくの
- ☐ staid 堅苦しい、形式ばった
- ☐ cautious 慎重な

2
- ☐ applaud 拍手する、称賛する
- ☐ align A with B AをBとそろえる、合わせる
- ☐ net-zero 実質ゼロ、ネットゼロ→排出される二酸化炭素と同量の二酸化炭素量を吸収・回収・利用して実質的にゼロにすること
- ☐ carbon dioxide emissions 二酸化炭素(CO_2)排出量
- ☐ predecessor 前任者
- ☐ promise 約束する
- ☐ reduce 削減する
- ☐ reach 達する
- ☐ carbon neutrality 炭素中立
- ☐ the second half 後半
- ☐ century 世紀
- ☐ reportedly 伝えられるところによると
- ☐ push 促す
- ☐ minister of economy, trade and industry 経済産業相
- ☐ environment minister 環境相
- ☐ outward 外向きの
- ☐ diplomatic 外交的な
- ☐ cost 代価、代償
- ☐ failure to *do* 〜しないこと
- ☐ lean forward 乗り出す
- ☐ issue 問題

Track 68

3　As the world's third largest economy, Japan has huge energy needs. Domestic supplies are limited—the country produces just 9% of its needs—so it relies on imports of fossil fuels, oil and coal primarily, but also natural gas, to satiate that appetite. Japan hoped nuclear energy would reduce reliance on imports and those highly polluting fuels, but the 2011 Fukushima nuclear power plant accident forced the government to shelve those plans.

4　The Basic Energy Plan, formulated in 2018, aims to make renewable energy a "main power source" responsible for 22 to 24% of overall power output by 2030. That goal has been achieved: The International Energy Agency estimates that renewable energy accounted for 23.1% of Japan's total energy generation mix in the first half of 2020. Nuclear-power plans have not fared as well. While anticipated to meet 20 to 22% of national needs by 2030, in 2019, nuclear plants produced just 7.5% of total power production.

Track 69

5　Japan must commit more fully to renewable energy sources—some say that as much as 50% of the country's supply—if it is to honor Mr. Suga's commitments. It is possible. The amount of electricity generated by renewable sources during the first half of 2020 grew 20% from the previous year, but those gains must be qualified. The increase is partly a result of a slowing economy and a concomitant decline in energy consumption.

3
- [ ] economy 経済国
- [ ] huge 巨大な、莫大な
- [ ] domestic supply 国内供給
- [ ] limited 限られた
- [ ] rely on ... …に頼る
- [ ] fossil fuel 化石燃料
- [ ] primarily 主として
- [ ] natural gas 天然ガス
- [ ] satiate 十分に満足させる
- [ ] appetite 欲求
- [ ] nuclear energy 原子力
- [ ] reliance 依存
- [ ] pollute 汚染を引き起こす
- [ ] nuclear power plant 原子力発電所
- [ ] force ... to *do* …に〜するよう強いる
- [ ] shelve 棚上げする

4
- [ ] Basic Energy Plan エネルギー基本計画
- [ ] formulate 策定する
- [ ] aim 狙いとする
- [ ] renewable energy 再生可能エネルギー
- [ ] power source 電源
- [ ] responsible for ... …を占める
- [ ] overall 全体の
- [ ] power output 電力出力、発電出力
- [ ] the International Energy Agency 国際エネルギー機関
- [ ] estimate 概算する、見積もる
- [ ] account for ... …を占める
- [ ] energy generation mix 発電の電源構成→電気の安定供給のため、複数のエネルギー源を組み合わせること
- [ ] fare well 順調に進む
- [ ] anticipate 予期する
- [ ] power production 電力生産

5
- [ ] fully 完全に
- [ ] source 源
- [ ] as much as ... …までも
- [ ] supply 供給
- [ ] honor 履行する
- [ ] amount 量
- [ ] grow 増える、伸びる
- [ ] previous year 前年
- [ ] gain 増加、増大
- [ ] qualify 修正を加える
- [ ] increase 拡大、増大
- [ ] partly 一部は、ある程度は
- [ ] result 結果
- [ ] slowing economy 景気減速
- [ ] concomitant 付随する
- [ ] decline 低下
- [ ] consumption 消費

6   Genuine, sustainable progress depends on changing economic incentives for energy production and use. That effort has been initiated with the decision to end investment in the construction of new coal-fired thermal plants both in Japan and overseas. Credit international pressure for that change, although it is not clear if or when Japan will shutter existing plants. Mr. Suga promised to "drastically" transform the country's policy on coal-fired power. The Ministry of Economy, Trade and Industry (METI) is supposed to develop an action plan by the year end with deadlines for specific targets to reach zero emissions. That will include the development of hydro and hydrogen supplies.

Track 70

7   The energy grid must be transformed. New modalities of power generation, delivery and storage are required. In addition to reducing the use of coal, the government is looking at solar, wind and hydrogen technologies. While cognizant of the public relations problems surrounding nuclear energy, the government is reluctant to reduce its commitment to that technology.

8   As important as changes to energy supply is a restructuring in energy demand. Production procedures must be changed across an array of industries. Steel production, for example, accounts for 47.6% of all industrial carbon dioxide emissions. Steel manufacturers should replace blast furnaces to reduce their carbon emissions. One option is electric-arc furnaces; another is using hydrogen rather than coal derivatives as European companies are.

6
- ☐ genuine 真の
- ☐ economic incentive 経済的誘因
- ☐ initiate 始める
- ☐ investment 投資
- ☐ coal-fired thermal plant 石炭火力発電所
- ☐ overseas 海外で
- ☐ credit A for B AにBの功績があると認める
- ☐ international pressure 国際的な圧力
- ☐ change 変革
- ☐ shutter 閉鎖する
- ☐ existing 既存の
- ☐ drastically 抜本的に
- ☐ transform 転換する
- ☐ the Ministry of Economy, Trade and Industry (METI) 経済産業省
- ☐ be supposed to *do* ～することになっている
- ☐ develop 作成する
- ☐ action plan 行動計画
- ☐ deadline 最終期限、締め切り
- ☐ specific 具体的な
- ☐ development 開発
- ☐ hydro 水力発電
- ☐ hydrogen 水素発電

7
- ☐ energy grid エネルギー供給網
- ☐ modality 様式
- ☐ delivery 送電
- ☐ storage 蓄電
- ☐ require 必要とする
- ☐ in addition to ... …に加えて
- ☐ solar 太陽光の
- ☐ cognizant of... …を認識している
- ☐ public relations 広報活動→ここでは、「一般大衆とのよい関係づくり」のこと
- ☐ surround 取り巻く
- ☐ reluctant 気乗りしない

8
- ☐ restructuring 再編成
- ☐ demand 需要
- ☐ procedure 手順、方法
- ☐ an array of ... さまざまな…
- ☐ industry 生産業、製造工業
- ☐ steel production 鉄鋼製造
- ☐ industrial 工業用
- ☐ steel manufacturer 鉄鋼メーカー
- ☐ replace 交換する
- ☐ blast furnace (製鉄所の)溶鉱炉、高炉
- ☐ option 選択肢
- ☐ electric-arc furnace 電気アーク炉
- ☐ derivative 誘導体

Track 71

9 Automobile manufacturers need to better promote electric vehicles. Japan, a leading maker of electric vehicles worldwide, has had anemic sales at home. Efforts have focused on hybrid and hydrogen vehicles. There were 300,000 electric vehicles on the road in Japan at the end of 2019—a little less than 1% of total market share. All industries must be attuned to ways that they can, in their operations and their products, reduce greenhouse gas emissions.

10 Much depends on the development of new technologies such as solar cells and storage capabilities (batteries), along with carbon recycling. There are signs of the needed transformation in Japanese thinking that sees changes not as problems but as possibilities. Green technologies are one of the most important opportunities businesses will have. Mr. Suga understands this moment. He argues that "We need to change our thinking and realize that structural changes in industry and society will lead to significant growth."

Track 72

11 The Japanese government should set aggressive targets and promote the transition to a green economy with tax incentives and subsidies for research and development as well as investment. Funds have been set aside and pilot projects are underway, but the pace must accelerate. Zero emissions and creating a carbon-neutral society will challenge Japan, but it is a challenge that must be met.

9
- ☐ automobile 自動車
- ☐ better さらにうまく、もっと十分に
- ☐ promote 販売を促進する
- ☐ electric vehicle 電気自動車
- ☐ leading 大手の
- ☐ worldwide 世界的に
- ☐ anemic 沈滞した
- ☐ at home 国内で
- ☐ effort 取り組み
- ☐ focus on ... …に集中する
- ☐ hybrid vehicle ハイブリッド車
- ☐ hydrogen vehicle 水素自動車
- ☐ a little less than ... …に満たない、…より少し少ない
- ☐ market share 市場占有率
- ☐ be attuned to ... …に合わせる
- ☐ operation 事業

10
- ☐ such as ... …のような
- ☐ solar cell 太陽電池
- ☐ battery 蓄電池
- ☐ along with ... …とともに
- ☐ carbon recycling 炭素リサイクル→地球温暖化の原因の二酸化炭素を資源として受け止め、回収・再利用によって排出量を削減すること
- ☐ sign 兆し
- ☐ transformation 転換
- ☐ not as A but as B AでなくBとして
- ☐ green technology 環境保全技術、グリーンテクノロジー
- ☐ opportunity 機会
- ☐ business 企業
- ☐ moment 機会
- ☐ argue 主張する
- ☐ significant 大きな、意義深い
- ☐ growth 成長

11
- ☐ aggressive 積極的な
- ☐ green economy グリーン経済、環境に優しい経済
- ☐ tax incentive 税制上の優遇措置
- ☐ subsidy 補助金
- ☐ funds 資金
- ☐ set aside 確保する
- ☐ pilot project 試験的プロジェクト
- ☐ underway 進行中で
- ☐ pace 速度
- ☐ accelerate 加速する

日本全体にさまざまな教訓を投げ掛けた都知事選

1 現職の知事に有利に働いたのは、新型コロナウイルス感染症（COVID-19）だったのだろうか。あるいは与党自民党が候補者を立てなかったからだろうか。日曜日の都知事選で小池百合子東京都知事が2期目を勝ち取ったのには、多くの理由があったかもしれない。

2 東京がわが国の首都であるにもかかわらず、精彩を欠いた選挙運動があまり国民の注目を集めることができなかったのは、残念なことだった。ただ、今回の選挙結果には国政にも関わる多くの意味合いがあるため、簡単に片付けてしまうべきではない。その学ぶべき教訓は、東京都民だけでなく、国民全体にとってのものだ。

3 COVID-19が選挙に与えた影響は甚大なものだった。小池氏は遊説を控え、公の場に姿を現すことを避けた。ほかの候補者もそれに倣った。小池氏はメディア団体主催のイベントに参加しないことが多かったため、選挙運動期間中の候補者間の白熱した政策論争はほとんどなかった。その結果、メディアによる選挙運動の報道は前回の都知事選挙と比べるとずっと少なく、有権者が候補者たちやその政策について知る機会が十分にはなかった。

4 今回の選挙では、選挙運動は主にインターネット上で行われた。オンラインでの選挙運動は若い有権者に訴求する可能性が大きく期待されたようであったが、現実には選挙関係のコンテンツに対するネット検索は、政治に強い関心がある層に限られていたようだ。

5 小池氏は頻繁にメッセージをインスタグラムやYouTubeといったソーシャルメディアに上げていたが、彼女のYouTube動画の多くはそれぞれ数千回の閲覧数を獲得しただけだった。小池氏がより広い層の人々に訴え掛けることに成功したとは言い難いだろう。

6 少なくともこの先数カ月はパンデミックが続く可能性が高いため、今後行われる選挙の候補者たちは自らの政策メッセージを有権者と直接触れ合うことなく届ける方法を模索する必要があり、メディアの側も人々がよりきちんと情報が知らされるように、選挙運動や候補者たちの政策の違いに関して報道していく努力をさらに強化していかなければならない。

7   今回の東京都知事選挙の投票率は55％で、前回の選挙から4.73％下がっている。これはここ10年間の多くの国政選挙よりはまだ高い数字ではあるものの、日本の首都の有権者の半数近くが投票しなかったことになる。

8   政治に対する無関心は東京に限られた現象ではないことは明らかだ。国会議員を選ぶ選挙の投票率は下がり続けている。投票率は2009年の衆議院議員選挙（野党民主党が政権を取るという結果になった選挙）の際の70％という高い数字から、2017年の総選挙では53.68％まで落ち込んだ。次の国政選挙までに、有権者を政治のプロセスに参加させるための努力がなされなければならない。

9   野党勢力が統一戦線を組めなかったことも、今回の小池氏の圧勝の一因となった。これは将来の国政選挙にも当てはまる教訓である。

10   東京の有権者の主な関心はCOVID-19の大流行によって引き起こされた危機をどのように乗り越えるかということだった。2,755人に対する朝日新聞の出口調査によると、64％が小池氏のコロナウイルス対策に賛成だと回答し、そのうち75％が小池氏に投票したという。一方で、34％が小池氏の採った方策には賛成しないと答えた。その中で、27％が元日本弁護士連合会会長の宇都宮健児氏に投票し、17％が日本維新の会の推薦を受けた元熊本県副知事の小野泰輔氏に票を投じた。小池氏は明らかに野党勢力の分裂に加え、現職であることの強みや、新型コロナウイルスの危機に関する最新情報を伝えるためにここ何カ月間かほぼ毎日テレビ出演していたことで得られたメディア露出といった恩恵を受けた。

11   また、今回の東京都知事の選挙運動では全国レベルでも同様に重要な多くの主要な問題に取り組むことができなかった。たとえば、候補者たちは東京オリンピック・パラリンピックについての意見を表明はしたが、保育施設増設の必要性や、膨れ上がる社会保障の費用、あるいはここ2カ月にわたって採られたウイルス対策で枯渇してきた、かつては潤沢にあった東京都の予備費をどのようにして増やすかといった問題に対する解決策については、論じられることはなかった。

12   国民の健康を守りながらどのように経済を再生していくかは地方行政および国政の両方のレベルにおいて政治指導者たちが取り組んでいかなければならない問題である。また、人口が急激に高齢化しているのは東京に限ったことではない。政治指導者たちはこうした喫緊の問題に取り組む方策を打ち出す必要があり、有権者は、自分たちが日本の針路を変えていく力を持っていることを自覚しなければならない。

(訳・注　小川)

再生可能エネルギー利用を増やす目標をさらに高めよ

1 日本はいまだに風力や太陽光発電などの再生可能エネルギーの利用に関し、ほかの多くの先進経済国や地域に大きく後れを取っている。日本政府は現在、再生可能エネルギーを推進するための一連の新しい方策を検討しており、その中には、洋上風力発電の拡大や、再生可能エネルギーの使用拡大にとって主なハードルの一つである送電システムへの接続ルールの見直しなどが含まれている。

2 わが国においてもより一層積極的に再生可能エネルギーを増やしていく目標を定めることによって、こうした取り組みを後押しする必要がある。具体的には、再生可能エネルギー産業への投資拡大を推進することや、気候変動との闘いの中でわが国のエネルギー政策を脱炭素化させようとする政府の関与を強調することである。

3 日本政府の基本的なエネルギー政策は、再生可能エネルギーを主要な電力供給源に変えていくことを求めている。ただ、2030年の電力供給構成の内訳における再生可能エネルギーが占める割合の目標値（全体の22〜24%）は、石炭火力発電所に構想されている26%と比べてすら低い。石炭火力発電所は、ほかの多くの先進工業国が段階的な廃止を計画しているが、それはほかのエネルギー源と比べて二酸化炭素などの地球温暖化ガスをより多く排出するからだ。2018会計年度において大規模水力発電を含む再生可能エネルギーがわが国の電力供給に占める割合は17%であり、これは2010年の9%から2倍近くに増えているが、いまだにヨーロッパの先進経済国や地域における水準には遠く及ばない。

4 東京電力ホールディングスの福島第一原子力発電所において2011年に炉心融解が起きたことを受け、わが国の原子力発電所のほとんどが稼働を停止されると、電力業界は原子力による発電量が失われた分（震災以前はわが国の電力需要の30%を供給していた）を補うため、石炭火力を含め、稼働する火力発電所を増やした。コストが格安であり、海外からの供給に関わる地理的リスクが低いことで好まれた石炭火力発電のシェアは2018年に32%に達し、天然ガスを使った発電所の38%に次いで第2位となった。

5 二酸化炭素排出を減らす世界的な取り組みに反して、日本が石炭に大きく依存していることから、近年ではますます国際的な風当たりが強くなってきている。日本政府は先月そのような批判に応え、「非効率的」とされる石炭火力発電所を段階的に廃止するという以前の公約を具体化した。わが国にある150基の石炭火力発電所のうち、120基は発電の面で効率が低い部類に分類されており、そのうち約100基は

2030年までに廃止または操業の一時停止により休止状態にすることになっている。

6 ところが、気候変動との闘いに対するこの取り組みの影響は、そうした数字が示唆するほどは大きくないかもしれない。使用中止が予定されている石炭火力発電所の大部分は古く、小出力の施設である。現在計画中または建設中のものも含め、存続予定のより「発電効率の高い」石炭火力発電所のほうがはるかに出力が大きいことから、ある環境保護団体の推計によると、日本の石炭火力発電所の発電量全体における正味の削減割合は約20%にしかならない。

7 実のところ、日本政府が2030年の電力供給配分における26%という石炭火力の割合を変えるとは考えられていない。「発電効率が高い」とされる石炭火力発電所でさえ、天然ガス使用の火力発電所と比べると2倍の二酸化炭素を排出すると言われていて、こうした石炭火力発電所の操業をこの先何十年も続けることで引き起こされる地球温暖化のリスクを指摘する向きも多い。

8 日本は温室効果ガスの排出を減らすために、発電時に二酸化炭素を排出しない原子力エネルギーに期待をかけてきた。ただ、2011年の福島原発事故の余波で稼働停止になった原子力発電所の再稼働はいまだに低調である。2018年の電力供給における原子力発電のシェアはたったの6%で、政府の2030年における目標値である20〜22%という数字には遠く及ばない。いまだに根強く残る安全性の懸念と、福島原発事故後増大した原子力発電所の稼働コストが原因で、停止中の原発の再稼働が近い将来大幅に加速する見通しはほんのわずかである。

9 原子力発電の将来の見通しがはっきりしないこと、そしてわが国が化石燃料を使って発電されたエネルギーに大きく依存し続けていることを考えると、日本政府は気候変動と闘うためのパリ協定に基づいた温室効果ガス排出削減に向けた取り組みを、改善できないままの状態でいる。各国が、地球温暖化の破滅的な影響を防止すべく5年ごとの自発的な計画の練り直しが迫られているにもかかわらずである。再生可能エネルギーの利用を大きく増やすことが、日本が自国の脱炭素化に向けた取り組みを加速する鍵を握っており、日本政府はエネルギー供給全体における再生可能エネルギー比率の目標を劇的に改善していくことによって、その取り組みを明確にしていく必要がある。

再生可能エネルギー利用を増やす目標をさらに高めよ

10 再生可能エネルギー源の利用がより普及しているほかの国々と比べ、日本ではそうしたエネルギーのコストが高いことに加え、気候条件に左右されやすい再生可能エネルギー源を使った発電が不安定であることが、わが国で再生可能エネルギーが普及しない理由としてしばしば挙げられてきた。こうした問題点をなかなか重い腰を上げない言い訳に使い続けることはもうやめて、われわれはそうした問題を克服し再生可能エネルギーのコストを下げるための技術革新を追求しなければならない。今こそわが国のエネルギーの構図を再構築する取り組みにおいて、方針を変えるときである。 　　　　　　　　　　　　　　　　　　　　　　（訳・注　小川）

政府中枢で求められる「働き方改革」

1 今月、衝撃的な調査結果が発表された。働き方のコンサルタント会社である株式会社ワーク・ライフバランスが3月から5月にかけて480人の公務員を対象に行った今回の調査によって、政府省庁の中で悲惨な数の官僚たちが、過労死を引き起こしかねないレベルで残業を行ってきていることが明らかになった。

2 特に新型コロナウイルスのまん延が原因で、官僚組織の中心地ともいえる東京・霞が関で働く、調査対象となった官僚の約40%が、月100時間以上という驚異的な残業時間を費やしている。

3 日本企業の多くの社員はかつて、家庭よりも会社で長い時間を過ごす「企業戦士」であると考えられていた。ところが今、「ワーク・ライフバランス」という概念が次第に民間企業に浸透してきており、加えて最近のパンデミックによってさまざまな形態の企業がテレワークその他の柔軟な働き方を受け入れざるを得なくなってきている。今こそ、効率を高めるために、政府職員の働き方を見直すときだ。

4 ワーク・ライフバランス社社長の小室淑恵氏とともに今回の調査結果を発表した小泉進次郎環境大臣は、厚生労働省の30代の官僚によって書かれた回答の一つを次のように引用している。「息子に『(平日に)初めてお父さんと一緒に夜ご飯が食べられた』と言われ、今まで人並みの親らしいことをしてあげられなくて、申し訳ない気分になり泣いてしまった。職員の家族の犠牲の上に成り立つ霞が関の働き方を再認識した」。

5 パンデミックが原因で、政府省庁の仕事量は増える一方だが、ステイホーム期間のおかげで官僚たちの中には家族と一緒に過ごす時間が増えた者がいることもまた事実である。

6 政府の官僚が働き方を変えられない大きな原因は、政治家たちがデジタル時代に順応することを拒み、夜遅くや朝早くであってもお構いなしに官僚たちにさまざまな状況説明を直接会って行うことを求め続けていることにある。ファクスを通じたメッセージや電話でのやりとりが政治家たちの日常のコミュニケーション手段として続いている。官僚たちは常にそうした国会議員たちからの要求にそのような旧態依然としたやり方で迅速に応えなければならないのである。

政府中枢で求められる「働き方改革」

7 今回の調査によると、回答者の80%が政治家への状況説明はオンラインではなく対面で行われていると答えており、一方で回答者の90%は政治家たちには官僚やその労働環境に対する配慮がないと感じているとコメントしている。

8 早急に紙の文書を使わない方式を採用すべきであるにもかかわらず、官僚たちの86%は、政治家たちにメッセージを送るためにはファクスを使わざるを得ないと述べている。

9 多くの政治家たちが対面でのコミュニケーションを志向する一方で、伝統的な業務のやり方もまた政府のあらゆる部署に根付いている。たとえば、紙の文書と印鑑の使用は政策承認の主要な手段となっており、その一方でオンライン会議ツールの利用はまだ限定的であり、官僚の中には自分はスカイプ以外のビデオ会議アプリを使えないとコメントしている者もいる。

10 政府を変えていくためには、国会のデジタル化もまた鍵となってくる。3月半ば、与党自由民主党の衆議院議員である鈴木隼人氏は、ほかの若手の国会議員とともにプロジェクトチームを立ち上げた。彼らは国会がオンライン会議ツールを採用し、国会議員たちが公務や出産、あるいは病気によって国会に登院できない場合はリモートで投票することを可能にするよう提言している。

11 橋本岳厚生労働副大臣と自見はなこ政務官が、コロナウイルスに見舞われたクルーズ船ダイヤモンド・プリンセス号に船内調査のため2月に横浜港で乗船した後、二人は隔離期間の2週間、国会に登院することができなかった。この間国家予算の審議が行われたが、両議員は参加することができなかったのである。

12 日本は新しい時代に見合った新しいルールと体制を作り上げていく必要がある。将来的に、女性議員が増えていけば国会の会期中に出産する議員が増えることになり、一方で障害を持つ人が国会議員になることも増えるかもしれない。また他方で、閣僚たちが重要な公務を執り行うために海外に行かなければならないこともあるだろう。憲法第56条は、本会議を開き議決するためには、3分の1以上の議員の出席を両議院に求めているが、もし国会議員が実際に国会に足を運ばずにオンラインで投票できれば、この規定を仮想空間（オンライン）上で満たすことができるだろう。

13 古い規則や慣習を新しいものに置き換えることは、官僚たちの労働環境の改善に資するだけではく、間違いなく多くの人々の時間と支出を節約し、それが最終的には納税者の払ったお金を節約することになるだろう。

14 世界は今回のパンデミックにより、途方もない難題に直面しており、日本はこれからの秋冬に起こりうる新型コロナウイルスとインフルエンザの二重の大流行に備える必要がある。政府における現在の非効率性に手を打たない限り、日本の政策決定の中心である国会が将来的な危機に迅速かつ効率的に対処することは極めて難しくなるだろう。　　　　　　　　　　　　　　　　　　　　（訳・注　小川）

菅政権発足、その先に待ち受ける難題

1 　菅義偉氏は水曜日に日本の第99代内閣総理大臣に選出され、体調不良で突然の退陣を余儀なくされた安倍晋三氏の後を継いだ。菅氏が選ばれたのは、政府と政策の安定と継続を確実にするためだ。日本が抱える不安定要素や増え続ける国内外の課題を踏まえると、その任務は一筋縄ではいかない。菅氏は長期にわたる輝かしいキャリアを通して有能で熱心な政治家であることを自ら示し、日本で史上最長在職日数（安倍首相の官邸での在職日数と同じ長さ）を誇る官房長官として有終の美を飾ると多くの人が考えていた。しかし、職業倫理を高く保つことは菅氏の新たな職務のほんの一部にすぎず、同氏はこの国の多くの課題を乗り越えるために必要なビジョンと創造性も持ち合わせなければならない。この点に関する評価の確実性は低い。

2 　菅氏の身の上話は注目に値する。たたき上げである彼は、政治的人脈のない秋田のイチゴ農家の息子で、法政大学の夜間部に通いながら自活していた。自民党議員の秘書として働き、のちに横浜市議会議員となり、そして国会議員に転身した。第一次安倍内閣の一員としては総務大臣を務めた。2007年に安倍氏が病気で官邸から去らざるを得なくなった後も引き続き彼に忠誠を尽くし、その献身ぶりが報われて2012年に安倍氏が首相として返り咲いた際には政権ナンバー2である内閣官房長官の職を与えられた。

3 　菅氏は今週行われた国会での投票で衆参両院において大多数の票を確保して首位の座を手にした。官邸入りが確実となったのは月曜日の自民党総裁選で勝利した結果で、それは同氏が534票中377票を獲得してさらなる信任を得た闘いであった。

4 　菅氏の選挙での勝利は保証されていた。当初はトップの座への意欲を否定していたが、その後、安倍氏の政策を継続するのに最適な人物として自民党幹部から抜てきされた。その意向は菅氏の陣営にはっきりと見てとれる。水曜日に発表された陣営では、安倍内閣の閣僚20人のうち8人は留任、さらに7人は横すべりまたは同じポストでの再入閣だった。政界権力者はポジションを維持した。党内第2派閥の会長である麻生太郎氏は副総理兼財務相を続け、自派トップの二階俊博氏は自民党幹事長としてとどまっている。安倍氏の弟である岸信夫氏が（自身初の閣僚ポストとして）防衛相に選ばれたことは、前任者を支持するという菅氏の主張（仮に疑問視されたことがあったとするなら）を裏付けている。

5 　菅氏にはあらゆる助けが必要となる。彼は圧倒されるような難題に直面している。

その多くは首相官邸の在任者である誰もが忙殺されるようなことだが、いくつかは彼だけに課されたものだ。当面の懸案事項は明らかである。新型コロナウイルス感染症（COVID-19）のまん延を抑制し、歴史的な縮小に見舞われている経済を再び軌道に乗せることだ。延期された2020年オリンピック・パラリンピックは、もう一つの優先事項だ。菅氏は規制緩和と構造改革を推進したいと述べているが、それはアベノミクスの矢筒に入っていたいわゆる「第三の矢」で、ほとんど立ち上がりを見せることがなかったとされるものだ。

6 外交政策では米国との関係を強固なものに保ち（特に緊密だった安倍氏とトランプ氏の関係を考えると難しい任務ではあるが）、その一方で中国との関係を安定・前進させねばならない。米中間の緊張や地政学的な大変革を踏まえるとどちらも難題だが、外交経験の乏しい菅氏には一層厳しい課題だ。こうした活動の場での安倍氏の取り組み、そして疑う余地のない成功事例と比べると、後継者の弱みがより目立つだろう。

7 菅氏のキャリアを特徴付けているのは、真摯な働きぶりと現実主義だ。彼は官僚組織の中で、そして官僚の間でどう立ち回ればよいかを知っている。しかしそうした努力は、誰かほかの人の政策に役立てるためだった。このことが彼にとって潜在的に最大の弱点となりうる。菅氏には自身の支持基盤がなく、派閥に入ったこともない。新たな取り組みを推進するには、安倍氏がそうであったように自民党最大派閥の一員であるか、あるいは小泉純一郎氏のように国民の支持を得ているときのほうが容易である。菅氏が立候補を表明して以来、努めて国民とのつながりを強調してきたことは、この領域でどれだけの仕事がなされるべきかを明確に示しただけにすぎない。

8 菅氏は、携帯電話料金の引き下げや保育所の増設、観光振興など、一般市民に影響を及ぼす問題の解決を好むと報じられているが、それは菅氏にとって極めて重要な国民との接点づくりに役立つはずだ。こうした問題に取り組むことは彼の最も重要な職務要件、つまり次の総選挙での自民党勝利を確実にすることに大きな役割を果たすだろう。安倍氏は自らの党を国政選挙で6連勝に導いた。

9 菅氏はCOVID-19による危機と経済の問題に焦点を当てて、選挙については考えていないと述べている。その優先順位は正しい。それらの問題にうまく対処することが国民の支持を獲得し、自らの党を勢いづけて選挙での勝利へとつなげるだろう。それは手腕と努力とかなりの運が求められる厳しい任務である。安倍氏は3つすべてを持っていた。菅氏も自身がそうであることを望んでいるに違いない。

（訳・注　宇都宮）

日米豪印の「自由で開かれたインド太平洋」戦略に期待

1 4カ国同盟（日本、米国、オーストラリア、インド）の外相が今週東京で会談し、その集まりの目的に関してさまざまな憶測が飛びかっている。それは修正主義的な中国に対して憂慮の念を持った国々による同国の封じ込めを目的とした会合であり、「自由で開かれたインド太平洋」地域推進のための組織であり、新生の地域安全保障構造の礎でさえある。「クアッド」と呼ばれるその会合はそれらすべてとなりうるが、先行きは不透明で、最終的な形や内容は今後の運営にかかっている。

2 4カ国戦略対話は2007年、安倍晋三首相の政権1期目に発足した。同会合は翌年、中国当局者から同会議は反中連合だと批判される中でオーストラリアが脱退したことや、参加国が目標と目的を共有しているのかという疑念が高まったりしたために頓挫した。

3 中国の行動に関する懸念の高まりが、4カ国を再挑戦へと駆り立てた。2017年にクアッドを復活させ、それ以来、さまざまなレベルで会合を重ねてきた。今週の会合は2回目の閣僚会議で、1回目は昨年、ニューヨークでの開催だった。

4 4カ国の政府はいずれも中国の行動に悩まされているが、米国が最も声高な批判者だ。マイク・ポンペオ米国務長官は自国の政権を代表して発言し、中国の「搾取、腐敗、抑圧」を非難して、その行動を「いじめ」だと見なした。日本の安全保障政策担当者も考えを同じくしているが、そういった露骨な言葉を使うことはないだろう。尖閣諸島をめぐる紛争を考えれば、中国は領土的な脅威をもたらしている国であり、地域的な優位性を求める修正主義勢力として広く認識されているが、それは、日本にとって高くつくことになる。

5 一方でオーストラリアが異議を唱えているのは、中国による南シナ海での人工島建設（これにはほかの国々も反対しているが）、国内政治への干渉、さらに中国への輸出品に対する制裁措置だ。その制裁は、オーストラリア政府がその干渉に不満を表明し、新型コロナウイルス感染症（COVID-19）流行の発生源について国際的な調査を求めた後に課された。インドはといえば、何十年にもわたって北の隣国と緊迫した関係にあり、数週間前にはヒマラヤ山脈にある両国間の国境紛争地で武力衝突が発生し、数十人の兵士が死亡する事態に発展した。

6 クアッド参加国の協力強化という目的を明確に表す軍事演習が注目を集めてきたが、議論はより広範囲に及んでおり、インフラ、電気通信システム（特に5G）、サイバーセキュリティー、知的財産保護、COVID-19の大流行への対応などの課題を含んでいる。今週の会合後、日本の茂木敏充外相は、クアッド参加国は開催の定例化とそれらの課題などに対する意見交換および協力に合意したと述べた。さらに、クアッドは他国との協力も拡大すべきだと同外相は提案したと報じられている。

7 議題と参加国を拡大するのはよい考えだが、ポンペオ氏が今週初め、グループを「制度化」し、その後「真の安全保障の枠組みを構築」して他の国々も「適切な時期に」参加すべきとした提案からはまだ程遠い。

8 それはしばらくは実現しないだろう。戦略的な連携と正式な安全保障の枠組みはまったくの別物だ。日本はオーストラリアやインドとの安全保障関係を大幅に強化してきたが、他国と安全保障を誓うといった点で法的な制約に直面している。（日本、オーストラリア、インドの）3カ国はいずれも中国との問題を抱えているが、地理的、経済的、政治的な実状を考慮した形での関係の修正も望んでいる。インドは地域的な包括的経済連携の貿易協定への参加を拒否したが、それはインド政府がどんな形であれ正式な束縛を嫌うことを思い起こさせるものである。

9 中国は事態をさらに難しくするだろう。中国外交部の汪文斌報道官は、「排他的な徒党を組む」ことや「第三者を標的にしたり、その利益を損ねたりする」ことをけん制し、「地域の国家間の相互理解と信頼に資する」「開放的で、包括的で透明性のある」協力を求めた。汪氏は、同盟の形成というポンペオ氏の意向を「ナンセンス」とはねつけ、こう付け加えた。「彼がその日を迎えることはないだろう。そして彼の後継者にもその日が来ることはない。なぜならその日は決して訪れないからだ」。

10 彼の言う通りかもしれない。だが、中国の行動は相変わらず心配の種だ。クアッド各国はほかの地域の政府同様、中国の行動を抑制する一番の方法は団結し、声を一つにすることだと理解している。だからといって、各国がまったく同じ政策を採用しなければならないということではない。参加国の政府が同じ目標に向かって努力し、互いの目的と戦略を理解している限り、微妙な差異や多様性の余地はある。

11 制度化された協力は別の目的も果たす。それは米国にもこの地域との関わりを強いるということだ。クアッドは、米国の意思決定を知る機会をもたらし、参加国にとって重要な懸念事項に関する米国政府の判断に影響を及ぼす機会を与える。

日米豪印の「自由で開かれたインド太平洋」戦略に期待

12 われわれは「自由で開かれたインド太平洋」地域への関与を共有しているが、その概念にはいまだ融通性があり、構想実現に向けた日本の国を挙げての取り組みはまだ進行中である。実現のための唯一の道は、地道で継続的なコミュニケーション、協力、連携だ。どのような形になるにせよ、クアッドはまさにそれを行うために不可欠な枠組みだ。　　　　　　　　　　　　　　　　　　　　　　（訳・注　宇都宮）

菅首相、伝統を守って東南アジアを最優先に

1 首相就任後の初めての外遊で、今週ベトナムとインドネシアという東南アジアの国々を歴訪した菅義偉首相は、前任者である安倍晋三氏の外交政策プログラムを継承したとして称賛された。2012年に首相の座に返り咲いたとき、安倍氏はベトナムを最初の外国訪問先としただけでなく、就任1年目に東南アジア諸国連合（ASEAN）の加盟10カ国すべてを訪れた。

2 この地域が日本政府の最優先事項になっている原因は中国にあるが、東南アジアはこれまでずっと日本にとって重要な利益関係のある地域の一つであった。わが国の首脳たちは、この地域の首脳からの支持と彼らとの友好的な関係を必要としていることを以前から認識している。中国政府が外交面と経済面でより手ごわい相手、および安全保障上の懸念をもたらす存在になるにつれて、そうした結び付きは今まで以上に大きな価値を帯びるようになってきた。

3 4日間に及ぶ2カ国歴訪は成功で、外交問題に関して経験が乏しいと広く見なされている首相にとって重要な成果であった。菅首相は、経済および安全保障上の懸念に関して具体的な結果を得るという、単純な方式を採用した。新型コロナウイルス感染症（COVID-19）の流行に由来する外交の制限を考慮すると、そこに焦点を合わせたことは理にかなっている。大規模なイベントが中止になり、人と人の交流や文化事業の機会が減った。

4 経済的な面では、菅首相は両国と日本の間の業務渡航を再開することでどちらの国とも合意に達したと伝えられており、各国がパンデミックから回復しようと奮闘する中で、これは最優先の課題であった。詳細は今後の協議を待たなければならないが、業務渡航を促進する必要性は、取り決めを成立させるための動機を提供するはずである。

5 菅首相が提唱するサプライチェーンの多様化も歓迎された。ほかの経済先進国と同様に、日本は製造工程の重要な結び目のつなぎ役として中国を頼ることを不安視している。日本企業が一部の業務を自国内に戻す、あるいは東南アジア全域により広く移転させるのを援助するために、日本政府は資金調達の仕組みを構築した（前者は注目を集めたものの、後者は注目されていない）。ベトナムおよびインドネシア政府は、日本企業による自国への投資の増加を歓迎している。

菅首相、伝統を守って東南アジアを最優先に

6 そうした流れは、菅首相がインドネシアのジョコ・ウィドド大統領に対して、特に高速鉄道などのインフラ事業を日本が継続すると約束する後押しにもなった。そうした計画により、同国は民間投資にとってより魅力的な場所になる。日本はまた、インドネシアに対して防災およびCOVID−19対策として500億円（4億7000万ドル）の円借款を提供すると発表した。

7 同様に重要なのが安全保障関連の合意である。ハノイでは菅首相とグエン・スアン・フック首相が、日本の防衛技術と装備品をベトナムに移転・輸出することに合意した。その点に関しても、詳細は今後協議される予定である。その合意は、ベトナム政府が沿岸警備隊の巡視艇6隻を建造するために366億3000万円を借り入れ、2025年10月までに引き渡されるとした、ベトナムと国際協力機構（JICA）の間の7月の契約を遂行するものである。

8 ジャカルタでは、菅首相とウィドド大統領が安全保障および防衛関係を強化し、より深めると約束した。南シナ海での安全保障協力体制を増強するとの2015年の合意に基づいて、両者は早期に外務および防衛大臣級の会談を開き、防衛関連の装備品および技術の売却に関する交渉を急ぐと述べた。

9 中国が菅首相の外遊を突き動かした力だと見ることは容易である。元外交官で現在は内閣官房参与の宮家邦彦氏は、今週に入ってジャパンタイムズ紙に掲載されたコラムで、誰もはっきりと名指しはしたくなかったとしても、会談では中国が「部屋の中のゾウ（全員が認識していても触れてはいけない存在）」であったと説明した。菅首相は発言の中で、南シナ海での「法の支配に逆行する」動きを非難する一方で、「ASEANと日本は基本的な原則を完全に共有している」と強調した。菅首相とフック首相は、「自由で開かれたインド太平洋」戦略で協力することに合意した。

10 その合意は受ける印象以下のものである。協力は承認していることを意味するものではないし、その違いが日本と、そのビジョンには参加していないと主張するASEAN各国政府とのギャップを端的に示している。その代わりに、東南アジア諸国は「ASEANのインド太平洋構想」を作り、インド太平洋地域という考え方は受け入れているものの、特定の戦略を支持することは周到に避けた。菅首相は、「法の支配、開放性、自由、透明性、包摂性をASEANの行動原理として力強くうたう」文書を「強く支持する」と述べることで、日本のビジョンとASEANの構想の間の差を埋めようと試みた。

11　包摂性の原則と一貫して（また、ASEAN各国政府の懸念を和らげ、中国政府の不満を抑えようとして）菅首相は、今月に入って東京で開かれた日本、米国、オーストラリア、インドによる非公式の集まりのクアッドには、環大西洋の安全保障機構であるNATOのアジア版になるといういかなる意図もないと語った。むしろ、日本とそのパートナーは「われわれの考え方を共有するいずれの国とも協力する用意がある」と述べている。

12　中国政府を怒らせたくないというASEAN各国政府の思いは、その経済において中国が果たす桁違いに大きな役割に端を発している。中国はASEANの全加盟国（ブルネイを除く）にとっての主要な輸入元であり、ASEANの全貿易に占める中国の割合は、2009年の11.6%から2019年の18%に増大した。各国政府は、中国政府がその貿易を影響力として、もしくは中国が同意しない決定に対して罰を与える手段として、行使するつもりなのではないかと警戒している。日本の貿易、投資、支援、援助は魅力的な対抗策であり、そして同時に、中国の修正主義への防止策にもなる。

13　ただし、そうした関係を中国との張り合いという視点で見るのは間違いである。菅首相が日本とASEANは「古い友人」で、その友情が両者の間の永続的かつ安定した関係の真の基盤であると強調したことは正しかった。菅首相とそのチームは、発する言葉が実行と政策において実現されることを確かなものにしなければならない。

（訳・注　桑田）

気候問題で菅氏が他国に倣って大胆な公約

1 先月の就任後初となる国会での所信表明演説で、菅義偉首相は、2050年までに温室効果ガスの排出ゼロを達成し、脱炭素社会を実現すると誓った。これは大胆な公約で、形式ばった慎重な政治家としての菅氏のイメージとはかけ離れたものだ。その目標の達成は容易ではないが、狙いは的確かつ実現可能である。

2 菅氏の演説は喝采を浴びたが、2050年までに二酸化炭素排出実質ゼロを達成すると同様の表明を行ったほかの120カ国に日本の歩調を合わせたにすぎない。前任の安倍晋三氏は、今世紀後半に温室効果ガス排出量を80%削減し、炭素中立を達成すると約束した。菅氏は、政府がこの問題に前向きに対処しなかった場合の外交的損失をともに熟知している梶山弘志経産相と小泉進次郎環境相（日本のエネルギー・環境政策の海外向けの顔である）によって、それより多くのことをするよう促されたと報じられる。

3 世界第3位の経済大国として、日本は莫大なエネルギー需要を抱えている。国内供給は限られており（自国の必要量のわずか9%しか生産していない）、その需要を満たすため、主に石油・石炭、それに天然ガスも含む化石燃料の輸入に依存している。輸入や、汚染度の極めて高いそれらの燃料への依存を原子力が減らすと日本は期待していたが、2011年の福島原発事故で、政府はこれらの計画の棚上げを余儀なくされた。

4 2018年に策定されたエネルギー基本計画は、2030年までに再生可能エネルギーを電力出力全体の22〜24%を担う「主力電源」にすることを目指すものだ。その目標は達成済みである。国際エネルギー機関（IEA）の概算では、再生可能エネルギーは、2020年上半期には日本の電源構成全体の23.1%を占めた。原子力計画はそれほど順調に進んではいない。2030年までに国の必要量の20〜22%を満たすと期待されているが、原発は2019年に総発電量の7.5%しか生産していない。

5 菅氏の公約を履行するというのであれば、日本は再生可能エネルギー源にもっと全面的に関わらなくてはならない（国の供給の実に50%を占めるべきだとの声もある）。それは可能である。再生可能エネルギー源により発電された電力量は、2020年上半期に前年比で20%増えたが、その増加分には修正を加えておかなければならない。この増大の幾分かは、経済減速とそれに伴うエネルギー消費の減少の結果だ。

6 真の持続可能な進歩は、エネルギー生産・使用に対する経済的誘因の改変にかかっている。この取り組みは、国内外の新規の石炭火力発電所建設への投資を終了する決定をもって開始された。日本が既存の発電所を閉鎖するのかどうか、もしくはそれがいつなのかは明らかでないとはいえ、その変革は国際的な圧力による成果だ。菅氏は石炭火力発電に関する国策を「抜本的に」変革すると約束した。経済産業省（METI）は、排出ゼロに達する具体的な諸目標の期限を定めた行動計画を年末までに策定することになっている。これには水力発電および水素発電による供給の開発が含まれる。

7 エネルギー供給網は変革されなければならない。発電、送電、蓄電の新しい様式が必須だ。石炭の使用量削減に加え、政府は太陽光、風力、水素技術に目を向けている。原子力を取り巻く広報活動上の問題を認識しながらも、政府は、その技術への関与を減らすことには消極的だ。

8 エネルギー供給の改変と同じく重要なのは、エネルギー需要の再編成だ。生産手順は、数多くの業界において変えなくてはならない。たとえば、鉄鋼製造は工業による二酸化炭素排出量全体の47.6%を占めている。鉄鋼メーカーは、炭素排出量を削減するために高炉を交換する必要がある。一つの選択肢は電気アーク炉だ。もう一つは、欧州の企業のように、石炭の誘導体ではなく水素を使用することである。

9 自動車メーカーは、電気自動車をもっとうまく販売促進させていく必要がある。世界的に電気自動車製造で先頭を走っている日本だが、国内販売は精彩に欠ける。販売努力はハイブリッド車と水素自動車に集中している。2019年末、日本の道路を走る電気自動車は（市場シェア全体の1%を少し下回る）30万台だった。すべての産業は、事業面でも製品面でも、温室効果ガスの排出削減ができる方法へと調整する必要がある。

10 多くのことが、炭素リサイクルとともに、太陽電池や蓄電能力（電池）などの新技術の開発にかかっている。変化を問題ではなく可能性と見なすといった、日本の考え方において必要とされている転換の兆しは見えている。グリーンテクノロジーは、企業が手にするであろう最も大切な機会の一つである。菅氏はこの節目を理解している。「私たちは発想を変え、産業と社会の構造変化が大きな成長につながることを認識する必要がある」と菅氏は主張する。

気候問題で菅氏が他国に倣って大胆な公約

11 日本政府は、積極的な目標を設定し、税制上の優遇措置や研究開発の補助金、そして同時に投資により、グリーン経済への移行を推進すべきである。資金は確保され、試験的プロジェクトが進行中だが、ペースを加速する必要がある。排出ゼロ、そして脱炭素社会の創設は日本にとって難問であるが、それは立ち向かわなければならない課題だ。

（訳・注　中村）

第3章 経済・財政

傘下のアント・グループが突然上場中止となったアリババ・グループ創業者の馬雲（ジャック・マー）氏
（写真は2015年のもの）

Ant's IPO gets stepped on

踏みにじられたアントの新規株式公開

November 12, 2020　　　　　●Tracks 73-77 / 訳 pp. 146-148

Track 73

1　The initial public offering (IPO) of Ant Group, originally scheduled for November 5, was much, much more than the coming-out party of a successful finance operation. The $37 billion offering would have been the world's largest and conferred a value of $316 billion on the Chinese financial giant. Listing in Hong Kong and Shanghai would show the world that Chinese companies had no need to go to New York to access capital; that the besieged special administrative region of Hong Kong remained a force to be reckoned with in international finance; and that China could produce corporate giants that mastered 21st century technologies.

2　With all that in the balance, Chinese authorities still pulled the plug on the IPO just two days before the scheduled event. Earlier that week, China's financial watchdogs published draft rules that significantly changed the regulatory environment, which in turn prompted suspension of the IPO. While that was the official explanation for the move, the decision was in fact an assertion of power and a reminder to Chinese business professionals that their government and not entrepreneurs—no matter how successful—are in charge.

中国の電子商取引大手アリババ・グループ傘下の金融サービス部門アント・グループが11月5日に予定していた世界最大規模の新規株式公開は、政府の介入により突然、延期となった。規制当局が新たに発表した規制案により、同社の株式公開の見通しは立っていない。

1
- □ [タイトル]Ant→中国の金融サービス会社アント・グループのこと
- □ [タイトル]IPO 新規株式公開→ initial public offering の略
- □ [タイトル]step on 踏みつける、圧迫する→アリ(ant)を踏むこととかけている
- □ coming-out party お披露目パーティー
- □ finance operation 資金繰り活動
- □ offering 提供
- □ confer A on B A を B に与える
- □ value 評価額
- □ financial giant 金融巨大企業
- □ listing 上場
- □ access 入手する
- □ capital 資本
- □ besieged 包囲された
- □ special administrative region 特別行政区
- □ remain 依然として…のままである
- □ force 有力な存在
- □ ... to be reckoned with 一目置かれるべき…
- □ corporate giant 大企業
- □ master 駆使する

2
- □ in the balance どちらとも決まっていない状態で
- □ authorities 当局
- □ pull the plug on ... …を突然中止する
- □ watchdog 監視機関
- □ publish 公表する
- □ draft rule 規制案
- □ significantly 大幅に
- □ regulatory environment 規制環境
- □ in turn 今度は
- □ suspension 停止
- □ move 措置
- □ in fact 実際には
- □ assertion 誇示
- □ reminder 注意喚起のメッセージ、再認識させるもの
- □ business professional 実業家
- □ entrepreneur 起業家
- □ no matter how ... どんなに…であろうとも
- □ in charge 掌握して

Track 74

3   By virtually all accounts, the draft regulations were released in response to a late October speech by Jack Ma, founder of Alibaba (which evolved into the Ant Group), in which he charged the main actors in China's financial system were neglecting the poor and most needy. He blasted China's banks, most of which are state-owned, for having "a pawnshop mentality," in which borrowers relied too heavily on collateral and other guarantees. Financial authorities used "yesterday's methods to regulate the future." As a result, growth was stunted because innovation was stifled. Mr. Ma was blunt: "Many of the world's problems," he said, were a result of "only talking about risk control, not talking about development, not thinking about young people's or developing countries' opportunities."

4   Ant sought to meet that need, matching borrowers with lenders who would provide small loans (sometimes called micro-lending), taking a small percentage of the loan from partner banks. (The name "Ant" was intended to signal a desire to serve the forgotten "little guy.") Ant insists it is a facilitator, not a lender; a technology company ("techfin"), not a financial institution ("fintech").

Track 75

5   Whatever sympathy regulators may have had for Mr. Ma's position dissipated after his October speech. Stung—the remarks were reportedly characterized by senior officials as "a punch in the face"—they released new regulations that require online micro-lending platforms to provide 30% of the funding of "joint loans" (an undefined term) that are offered through their platforms. Currently, Ant funds only 2% of the 1.7 trillion yuan ($256.9 billion) in consumer loans it has out. That huge increase would severely limit Ant's business prospects and forced suspension of the IPO.

3
- □ by all accounts 誰の目から見ても
- □ virtually ほとんど
- □ regulation 規制
- □ release 発表する
- □ in response to ... …を受けて
- □ Jack Ma 馬雲（ジャック・マー）
- □ founder 創業者
- □ Alibaba アリババ→中国の電子商取引最大手
- □ evolve into ... …へと発展する
- □ charge 非難する
- □ main actor 中心的存在
- □ neglect なおざりにする
- □ the poor 貧困層
- □ the most needy 最も困窮している人々
- □ blast 激しく非難する
- □ state-owned 国有の
- □ pawnshop 質屋
- □ mentality 考え方
- □ borrower 借り手
- □ rely on ... …に依存する
- □ collateral 担保
- □ guarantee 保証
- □ stunt 阻む
- □ innovation 革新
- □ stifle 抑える
- □ blunt 単刀直入の
- □ development 発展、展開

4
- □ seek to *do* ～しようと努める
- □ meet a need 需要に応える
- □ match A with B AをBに引き合わせる
- □ lender 貸金業者
- □ small loan 小口融資
- □ signal 示す
- □ serve …の役に立つ
- □ little guy 小さな存在、弱者
- □ facilitator 世話役
- □ techfin →ICT（情報通信技術）に金融機能を加えた会社
- □ financial institution 金融機関
- □ fintech →金融会社がそのシステム上にICTを採用した会社

5
- □ sympathy 共感
- □ regulator 規制当局
- □ position 見解
- □ dissipate 消える
- □ sting 感情を害する
- □ remark 発言
- □ reportedly 報道によると
- □ characterize A as B AをBであると見なす
- □ senior official 高官
- □ provide 提供する
- □ funding 資金
- □ joint loan 共同融資
- □ undefined 定義されていない
- □ term 用語
- □ yuan 元→中国の通貨単位
- □ consumer loan 消費者ローン
- □ huge 大きな
- □ severely 厳しく
- □ prospect 見通し、将来性

6 The Chinese government is right to worry about the stability of its financial system. Ant's leverage is staggering and it is not the only Chinese company with that exposure. According to one estimate, 13% of the country's financial institutions can be considered "high risk." The Western world knows well the price of complacency and indifferent rule-making in the financial sector: The Great Recession was the result.

Track 76

7 Chinese President Xi Jinping rightly identified financial security as a national security concern in 2017. Earlier this month, the People's Bank of China, the country's central bank, released its "China Financial Stability Report," and underscored the risks involved and the need for a more comprehensive and coherent regulatory framework.

8 But the argument that the new regulations were a reminder of the authority of the Chinese government is reinforced by other developments. In September, the General Office of the Central Committee of the Communist Party of China called for efforts to "guide" private enterprises to "improve their corporate governance structure and explore the establishment of a modern enterprise system with Chinese characteristics"—in other words, to increase party influence in private companies and better direct the private sector toward government objectives.

6
- ☐ stability 安定性
- ☐ leverage 借入資本利用
- ☐ staggering 驚異的な、莫大な
- ☐ exposure リスクにさらされる度合い
- ☐ estimate 試算
- ☐ consider 見なす
- ☐ the Western world 欧米諸国
- ☐ price 代償
- ☐ complacency 自己満足
- ☐ indifferent 無関心な
- ☐ rule-making 規則の制定
- ☐ financial sector 金融部門
- ☐ the Great Recession →米国のサブプライムローン危機に端を発した世界的金融不況

7
- ☐ Xi Jinping 習近平
- ☐ rightly 当然のことながら
- ☐ identify A as B AをBであると見なす
- ☐ national security 国家安全保障
- ☐ concern 懸念
- ☐ People's Bank of China 中国人民銀行
- ☐ central bank 中央銀行
- ☐ China Financial Stability Report 中国金融安定性報告書
- ☐ underscore 強調する
- ☐ ... involved 内在する…
- ☐ comprehensive 包括的な
- ☐ coherent 一貫した
- ☐ framework 枠組み

8
- ☐ argument 主張
- ☐ authority 権限、権威
- ☐ reinforce 強固にする
- ☐ the General Office 中央弁公庁
- ☐ the Central Committee of the Communist Party of China 中国共産党中央委員会
- ☐ call for ... …を要求する
- ☐ effort 取り組み
- ☐ guide 指導する
- ☐ private enterprise 民間企業
- ☐ improve 改善する
- ☐ corporate governance structure 企業統治体制
- ☐ explore 模索する
- ☐ establishment 構築
- ☐ characteristic(s) 特色
- ☐ in other words 言い換えれば、つまり
- ☐ influence 影響力
- ☐ direct A toward B AをBへと導く
- ☐ objective 目標

Track 77

9 In November, the Central Commission for Comprehensively Deepening Reforms, an agency headed by President Xi Jinping, called for state-owned enterprises to be "stronger, better and bigger" so that they could play a more effective role in the national economy. And earlier this week, the State Administration for Market Regulation released guidelines that for the first time define anti-competition practices among internet companies, effectively setting limits on what has become a market of behemoths. All these moves strengthen state power over the private sector.

10 Ant may yet issue its IPO. The draft regulations will have to be finalized, however, and the company must then ensure its compliance with those rules. The first step alone could take as long as a year. During that time, Mr. Ma, along with other Chinese entrepreneurs and anyone that wants to do business in China, will have time to think about their prospects—and their limits.

9
- ☐ Central Commission for Comprehensively Deepening Reforms 中央全面深化改革領導小組
- ☐ agency 機関
- ☐ headed by ... …が代表を務める
- ☐ so that ... …するように
- ☐ play a role 役割を果たす
- ☐ effective 効果的な
- ☐ national economy 国家経済
- ☐ State Administration for Market Regulation 国家市場監督管理総局
- ☐ for the first time 初めて
- ☐ anti-competition practice 反競争的行為
- ☐ among …の間で
- ☐ effectively 事実上
- ☐ set a limit on ... …に制約を設ける
- ☐ behemoth 巨大企業
- ☐ strengthen 強化する
- ☐ state power 国家の権力

10
- ☐ yet やがては
- ☐ issue 発行する
- ☐ finalize 成立させる
- ☐ then それから
- ☐ ensure 確実にする
- ☐ compliance with ... …の順守
- ☐ alone それだけで
- ☐ as long as …もの長い間
- ☐ along with …とともに

RCEP: Big numbers, bigger potential

RCEP：大きな数、より大きな将来性

November 19, 2020　　　　　　●Tracks 78-83 / 訳 pp. 149-151

Track 78

1　The signing last Sunday of the RCEP, the Regional Comprehensive Economic Partnership, is a significant achievement. Eight years of negotiation yielded an agreement whose members account for 2.2 billion people and about 30% of the global economy. By those measures, it is the largest trade deal in history.

2　More significantly, the RCEP lays a foundation for future economic and political integration in Asia and it is doing so without the United States. Decisions by U.S. administrations to maintain distance from this trade pact and the Comprehensive and Progressive Agreement for Trans-Pacific Partnership (CPTPP) were a mistake— although they can be remedied. In the meantime, the U.S. absence obliges Japan to show leadership to direct both agreements toward integration, openness, good governance and the rule of law.

Track 79

3　RCEP negotiations began in 2012 and proceeded fitfully. Conclusion of the CPTPP, first as the Trans-Pacific Partnership and then in a revised form in 2018, spurred RCEP governments to wrap up their talks. Agreement might have been possible a year ago but India then decided to withdraw from the pact fearing it would unleash a flood of Chinese imports. After recognizing that this was not a negotiating tactic and Delhi would not return, the remaining 15 governments—10 members of ASEAN (Brunei, Cambodia, Indonesia, Laos, Malaysia, Myanmar, the Philippines, Singapore, Thailand and Vietnam) and Japan, China, South Korea, Australia and New Zealand—finalized the deal.

8年間に及ぶ長い交渉の末に、RCEPが署名された。日中韓を含む15カ国による経済的枠組みがアジア地域に誕生した意義は大きいが、真の成果を得るためには、不参加を表明した米国とインドを再び取り込むことができるかが鍵を握っている。

1
- ☐ [タイトル]RCEP 地域的な包括的経済連携→(the) Regional Comprehensive Economic Partnership の略
- ☐ [タイトル]potential 将来性
- ☐ signing 署名
- ☐ significant 意義深い
- ☐ achievement 成果
- ☐ negotiation 交渉
- ☐ yield 生む、結果を出す
- ☐ account for ... …を占める
- ☐ global economy 世界経済
- ☐ measure 尺度
- ☐ trade deal 貿易協定

2
- ☐ significantly 意義深いことに
- ☐ lay a foundation 基盤を築く
- ☐ integration 統合
- ☐ administration 政権、政府
- ☐ maintain distance 距離を保つ
- ☐ pact 協定
- ☐ the Comprehensive and Progressive Agreement for Trans-Pacific Partnership 環太平洋
- パートナーシップに関する包括的及び先進的な協定
- ☐ remedy 修正する
- ☐ in the meantime その一方で
- ☐ oblige ... to *do* …に～することを余儀なくさせる
- ☐ direct 方向付ける
- ☐ governance 統治
- ☐ the rule of law 法の支配

3
- ☐ proceed 進行する
- ☐ fitfully 断続的に
- ☐ conclusion 締結
- ☐ the Trans-Pacific Partnership 環太平洋パートナーシップ
- ☐ revised 修正された
- ☐ spur ... to *do* …が～するのを後押しする
- ☐ wrap up ... …をまとめる
- ☐ withdraw 離脱する
- ☐ unleash 解き放つ、引き起こす
- ☐ a flood of ... 大量の…
- ☐ import 輸入品
- ☐ recognize 認識する
- ☐ negotiating tactic 交渉戦術
- ☐ Delhi インド政府
- ☐ remaining 残りの
- ☐ ASEAN→東南アジア諸国連合 (Association of Southeast Asian Nations)の略称
- ☐ finalize まとめる、仕上げる

4   While the headline numbers are large, actual economic benefits are less substantial. CPTPP reduces tariffs more than the RCEP, and most signatories have bilateral agreements with low tariff rates; members of ASEAN already trade freely among themselves. One reason the deal is attractive is that it simplifies the "noodle bowl" of existing trade agreements. According to one estimate, RCEP will by 2030 add $186 billion to the global economy—less than a drop in the bucket of a global economy that already exceeds $80 trillion—and 0.2% to the GDP of its members.

Track 80

5   It is the symbolism of the deal that matters most. RCEP is reaffirmation of the signatories' commitment to trade liberalization and deeper integration at a time when governments are putting up barriers and reverting to protectionism. It is the first trade agreement that brings together China, Japan and South Korea, the world's second, third and twelfth largest economies, respectively. That will pay real dividends for Japan. Currently, 8% of Japanese goods exported to China are not subject to tariffs; under RCEP, that number will climb to 86%, transforming the terms of trade. China's Ministry of Finance called the change "a historic breakthrough."

6   The inclusion of those three countries within a single regional economic framework in combination with the simplification of the current trade patchwork gives RCEP its real significance and its greatest potential. It could provide the foundation of a coherent economic unit like North America or, with greater ambition and integration, like the European Union.

4
- □ headline number 見出しの数字→新聞の見出しで目を引くために扱われる数字のことで、必ずしも実態を表していないというニュアンスがある
- □ substantial かなりの
- □ tariff 関税
- □ signatory 署名国
- □ bilateral 二国間の
- □ simplify 簡素化する
- □ noodle bowl ヌードルボウル→自由貿易協定や多国間貿易協定が混在する状態

のこと。欧米では spaghetti bowl(スパゲッティボウル)と言う
- □ existing 既存の
- □ estimate 見積もり、試算
- □ a drop in the bucket 大海の一滴→直訳すると「バケツの中の一滴」で、ほんのわずかな量という意味
- □ exceed 上回る
- □ GDP →Gross Domestic Product(国内総生産)の略

5
- □ symbolism 象徴的意義
- □ matter 重要である
- □ reaffirmation 再確認
- □ commitment 深い関与
- □ liberalization 自由化
- □ put up ... …を築く
- □ barrier 障壁
- □ revert to ... …に逆戻りする
- □ protectionism 保護主義
- □ bring together ... …を一つにする
- □ respectively それぞれ
- □ pay dividends 大きな利益をもたらす
- □ currently 現在のところ
- □ goods 品物、商品
- □ be subject to ... …の対象になる
- □ climb to ... …に達する
- □ transform 一変させる
- □ the terms of trade 交易条件
- □ Ministry of Finance (中国の)財政部
- □ breakthrough 躍進

6
- □ inclusion 含めること
- □ framework 枠組み
- □ in combination with ... …と合わせて
- □ simplification 簡素化
- □ patchwork 寄せ集め、継ぎはぎ状態
- □ significance 重要性、意義
- □ provide 提供する
- □ coherent 結束した
- □ economic unit 経済単位
- □ North America →ここでは、米国、カナダ、メキシコによる北米自由貿易協定(North American Free Trade Agreement)を指す
- □ ambition 野心
- □ the European Union 欧州連合

Track 81

7   The deal creates single rules of origin for the 15 member states, which will greatly facilitate internal trade: One piece of paper will allow goods to be exchanged among all members. While most of the region's products are consumed elsewhere in the world, RCEP is expected to accelerate development of the internal market so that Asians are producing for themselves. That would constitute a historical shift in the working of the global economy.

8   RCEP is widely viewed as a victory for China. That is true but only insofar as it is a win for Japan or any other signatory. The agreement was proposed and driven by ASEAN. China is large and will shape RCEP's future, but so too will Japan. The real measure of a country's influence will be evident as members meet as stipulated by the pact to develop and refine standards, or add new members. Especially important will be rules and regulations regarding new technologies and their uses, such as e-commerce and control of data. Japan must be especially attentive to and aggressive in this process.

Track 82

9   Tokyo's role will be facilitated by its membership in the CPTPP; six other countries are also members of the two agreements. Tokyo should work closely with them to ensure that RCEP evolves toward greater openness and liberalization, in the direction of the larger, more comprehensive agreement; ideally, there would eventually be a merger with CPTPP.

7
- rules of origin 原産地規則→輸入される貨物の原産地を決めるための規則
- member state 加盟国
- facilitate 促進する
- internal 内部の、域内の
- exchange 取引する
- consume 消費する
- be expected to *do* ～すると期待される
- accelerate 加速する
- development 発展
- constitute 相当する
- historical shift 歴史的転換
- working 仕組み

8
- be widely viewed as ... …だと広く見なされる
- insofar as ... …である限り
- propose 提案する
- drive 主導する
- shape （方向性を）決定する
- influence 影響力
- evident 明らかな
- stipulate 規定する
- refine 改善する
- especially とりわけ
- rules and regulations 規約
- regarding …に関して
- e-commerce 電子商取引
- be attentive to ... …に注意を払う
- aggressive 積極的な
- process プロセス、過程

9
- membership 加盟国であること
- closely 緊密に
- ensure 確実にする
- evolve 発展する
- in the direction of ... …の方向に
- ideally 理想的には
- eventually いずれは
- merger 合併

10 Equally important for Japan is convincing the United States to return and recommit to Asia's economic institutions. The U.S. decision to withdraw from the CPTPP, then known as the TPP, was a strategic blunder, greatly diminishing Washington's influence in the region. (President Trump's rejection of regional summitry contributed to this decline.) President-elect Joe Biden understands the need to engage. He recognizes that influence derives from rule making and the U.S. must join institutions to shape their future and that of the region as a whole.

`Track 83`

11 He also knows that he must first tackle COVID-19 and rebuild his country's competitiveness. Americans value free trade and globalization, but they also want their leaders to reconnect with the middle class and help secure their future. Japan should help the United States better understand that the more deeply it is integrated with the region, the more prosperous and secure it will be. That has been Japan's course in the postwar era, one that has been encouraged by successive U.S. administrations. Now it is time to offer the same wise counsel.

10
- [ ] convince 説得する
- [ ] recommit to ... …に再び関与する
- [ ] Asia's economic institutions アジアの経済機構→RCEPとCPTPPを指す
- [ ] then known as ... 当時は…として知られていた
- [ ] strategic 戦略的な
- [ ] blunder 大失態
- [ ] diminish 減らす
- [ ] rejection 拒否
- [ ] summitry 首脳会議への参加
- [ ] contribute to ... …に寄与する、…の一因になる
- [ ] decline 減少、衰退
- [ ] president-elect 次期大統領→-electは「(就任前の)選ばれた」の意
- [ ] engage 関与する
- [ ] derive from ... …に由来する
- [ ] rule making 規則制定
- [ ] as a whole 全体として

11
- [ ] tackle 取り組む
- [ ] COVID-19 新型コロナウイルス感染症
- [ ] rebuild 立て直す
- [ ] competitiveness 競争力
- [ ] value 尊重する
- [ ] globalization グローバリゼーション、グローバル化
- [ ] reconnect with ... …と再びつながる
- [ ] the middle class 中産階級
- [ ] secure 確実なものにする→6行目では形容詞で「安定した」の意
- [ ] be integrated with ... …と統合される
- [ ] prosperous 繁栄した
- [ ] postwar 戦後の
- [ ] encourage 奨励する
- [ ] successive 連続した、歴代の
- [ ] counsel 助言

踏みにじられたアントの新規株式公開

1　当初は11月5日に予定されていたアント・グループの新規株式公開（IPO）は、成功を収めた資金繰り活動のお披露目パーティーよりも数段意味のあるものだった。370億ドルの株式の提供は世界最大規模で、その中国系金融大手に3160億ドルの評価額をもたらすはずだった。香港と上海で上場していれば、中国企業は資金調達のためにニューヨークに頼らずに済むこと、包囲された状態にある香港特別行政区が依然として国際金融で一目置かれる存在であること、そして、中国は21世紀のテクノロジーを駆使した大企業を輩出できることを世界に知らしめただろう。

2　それらのことすべてがまだどちらか決まっていない状況であったが、中国当局はそれでも予定日のわずか2日前にIPOを突然中止した。今週に入って中国の金融監視機関は規制環境を大幅に変更した規制案を公表し、次にはその案がIPOの停止を引き起こすこととなった。それが今回の措置の公式な説明だったものの、その決定は実際には権力の誇示であり、権限を掌握しているのは政府であって（どんなに成功を収めていても）起業家ではないことを中国人実業家らに注意喚起するメッセージだった。

3　ほとんど誰の目から見てもこの規制案は、アリババ（のちにアント・グループへと発展）の創業者、馬雲氏による10月下旬の演説を受けて発表されたものだ。その中で彼は、中国の金融制度の中心人物たちは貧困層および最も困窮している人々をなおざりにしていると非難した。中国の銀行（そのほとんどが国有である）は「質屋的思考」を持っているとして激しい非難を浴びせたが、そこでは借り手が担保やその他の保証に過度に依存している。金融当局は「昨日の手法で未来を規制」した。その結果、革新が阻害されたために、成長が妨げられた。馬氏は単刀直入にこう述べた。「『世界の問題の多くは、リスク管理の話ばかりして発展を語らず、若者や発展途上国の機会について考えないこと』によるものである」。

4　アントはそのようなニーズに応えようと（マイクロ・レンディングとも呼ばれる）小口融資を提供する貸金業者と借り手を引き合わせ、その融資のわずかな割合をパートナー銀行から受け取った（「アント」という名前は、忘れ去られた「小さな存在」の役に立ちたいという願いを伝えることを意図したものだ）。アントは自社について、貸し手ではなく世話役であり、金融機関（いわゆる「フィンテック企業」）ではなくテクノロジー企業（いわゆる「テックフィン企業」）であると主張している。

5　規制当局が馬氏の見解に共感するところがこれまでにあったとしても、それは10月の演説後には消えてなくなった。その発言は高官らに「顔面への一撃」と見なされたと報じられており、感情を害した当局は新たな規制を発表した。それは、オンライン経由の小口融資プラットフォームに対して、自社のプラットフォームを通じて提供される「共同融資」（定義されていない用語）の資金のうち3割を出すことを求めるものだ。現在、アントは貸し出した1兆7000億元（2569億ドル）の消費者ローンの2%しか資金を出していない。その大幅な増加はアントの事業見通しを厳しく限定するもので、IPOの停止を余儀なくさせた。

6　中国政府が金融システムの安定性について懸念するのは当然だ。アントの借入資本利用は驚異的で、そのぐらいの脆弱性を持つ中国企業はほかにもある。ある試算によると、同国の金融機関の13%が「高リスク」状態であると見ることができるという。欧米諸国は、金融部門におけるひとりよがりと無頓着なルール作りの代償をよくわかっている。世界的金融不況がその結果だった。

7　中国の習近平国家主席が2017年に金融の安全性を国家の安全保障上の関心事と見なしたのは当然のことだった。今月に入って、中国の中央銀行である中国人民銀行は「中国金融安定性報告書」を発表し、内在するリスクと、より包括的で一貫した規制枠組みの必要性を強調した。

8　しかし、新たな規制は中国政府の権限を再認識させるものだったとの主張は、その他の展開によって強固なものとなる。9月に中国共産党中央委員会の中央弁公庁が呼び掛けた取り組みは、民間企業を「指導」して「企業統治体制を改善し、中国の特色を持った近代的な企業システムの構築を模索する」こと、つまり民間企業における党の影響力を高め、民間部門を政府が目標とする方向へともっとうまく導くことだった。

9　11月には、習近平国家主席が率いる中央全面深化改革領導小組が国有企業に対し、国家経済でより効果的な役割を果たせるよう、「より強く、よく、大きく」なることを求めた。また今週に入り、国家市場監督管理総局がインターネット企業間の反競争的行為を初めて定義したガイドラインを発表し、今や巨大企業が占める市場に事実上の制約を設けた。これらの展開はすべて、民間部門に対する国家の権力を強化するものだ。

踏みにじられたアントの新規株式公開

10 アントはやがてはIPOを発行する可能性がある。だが今後規制案がまとめあげら
れなければならず、同社はその後、その規則を確実に順守しなければならない。
その第一歩だけでも1年もの期間を要する可能性がある。その間、馬氏はほかの
中国人起業家や中国でビジネスをすることを望むあらゆる人たちとともに、自分た
ちの将来性、そして限界について考える時間を持つことになるだろう。

（訳・注　宇都宮）

RCEP：大きな数、より大きな将来性

1 先週日曜日のRCEP（地域的な包括的経済連携）協定の署名は意義深い成果である。8年間の交渉の末に、加盟国の人口が合計22億人、世界経済の約30%を占める合意が誕生した。そうした尺度で見ると、それは歴史上で最大の貿易協定に当たる。

2 より意義深いのは、RCEPがアジアにおける将来の経済的および政治的統合の基盤を築き、しかもそれを米国抜きで進めていることである。この貿易協定と、環太平洋パートナーシップに関する包括的及び先進的な協定（CPTPP）から距離を置くという米国政府の決定は、誤りであった（ただし、修正される可能性はある）。その一方で、米国の不在により、両協定を統合、開放性、よい統治、法の支配へと方向付ける上で、日本はリーダーシップを示すことを余儀なくされている。

3 RCEPの交渉は2012年に始まり、断続的に進行した。当初は環太平洋パートナーシップとして、その後2018年の修正版によるCPTPPの締結は、RCEP各国政府に交渉をまとめるよう後押しした。合意は1年前に可能であったかもしれないが、中国からの輸入品の大量流入をもたらすのではないかと恐れたインドが、その時点で協定からの離脱を決定した。これが交渉戦術ではなく、インド政府には戻るつもりがないと認識した後、残る15カ国（ASEAN加盟国であるブルネイ、カンボジア、インドネシア、ラオス、マレーシア、ミャンマー、フィリピン、シンガポール、タイ、ベトナムの10カ国と、日本、中国、韓国、オーストラリア、ニュージーランド）の政府が協定をまとめた。

4 報道される数字は大きい一方で、実際の経済的な恩恵はそれほど多くはない。CPTPPのほうがRCEPよりも関税を下げているし、ほとんどの署名国は低い関税率で二国間協定を結んでいる。ASEANの加盟国間ではすでに自由に貿易が行われている。協定が魅力的だという一つの理由は、既存の貿易協定の「ヌードルボウル現象」を簡素化することにある。ある試算によると、RCEPは2030年までに世界経済に1860億ドル（これはすでに80兆ドルを上回る世界経済の中では、大海の一滴にも満たない）を加算し、加盟国のGDPを0.2%増やすことになるという。

5 最も肝心なのは協定の持つ象徴的意義である。各国政府が障壁を築き、保護主義へと逆戻りしつつある時代において、RCEPは貿易の自由化とより深い統合に対する署名国の関与を再確認するものだ。中国、日本、韓国という、それぞれ世界2位、3位、12位の経済大国が一つにまとまる初めての貿易協定に当たる。そのことは

RCEP：大きな数、より大きな将来性

日本に真の利益をもたらすであろう。現在、中国に輸出される日本製品の8%には関税がかかっていない。RCEPが発効すると、その数字は86%に増加し、交易条件が一変する。中国の財務部はその変化を「歴史的な躍進」と評した。

6 その3カ国を一つの地域的な経済の枠組みに含めることは、現在の貿易慣行の寄せ集め状態の簡素化と合わせて、RCEPに真の重要性と最大の将来性をもたらす。北アメリカの協定のような、あるいはより大きな野心と統合があれば欧州連合のような、結束した経済単位の基盤を提供するかもしれない。

7 協定は加盟15カ国に対して単一の原産地規則を設定しており、そのことは域内貿易を大いに促進するであろう。1枚の紙があれば、すべての加盟国の間で品物の取引が可能になる。この地域の生産物の大半は世界のほかの場所で消費されているものの、RCEPは域内市場の発展を加速し、アジア人が自分たちのために生産するようになることが期待されている。そのことは世界経済の仕組みにおける歴史的な転換となるであろう。

8 RCEPは中国にとっての勝利と広く見なされている。それは事実だが、日本ないしほかのどの署名国にとっても勝利であるという限りにおいてのみである。協定はASEANによって提案され、主導された。中国は大国で、RCEPの将来を決定付けることになるが、それは日本も同じであろう。国の影響力の真の尺度は、規範を形成・改善したり、新たな加盟国を加えたりするために、協定が規定するところに従って加盟国が集まるときに明らかになるだろう。とりわけ重要なのは、電子商取引やデータの管理などの、新しい技術やその使用に関する規約であろう。日本はこのプロセスに対して特に注意を払い、積極的でなければならない。

9 日本政府の役割はCPTPPの加盟国であることで容易になるであろう。ほかに6つの国がこの2つの協定の加盟国になっている。RCEPがより大きな開放性と自由化に向けて、より広くより包括的な協定の方向へと確実に発展するよう、日本政府はそうした国々と緊密に協力するべきである。いずれはCPTPPとの合併となれば理想的である。

10 日本にとって等しく重要なのは、アジアの経済機構に復帰して再び深く関わるよう、米国を説得することである。当時はTPPとして知られていたCPTPPから離脱するという米国の決定は戦略的な大失策で、米国政府のアジア地域での影響力を大幅

に減らすことになった（トランプ大統領の地域首脳会議への参加拒否がこの衰退に寄与した）。ジョー・バイデン次期大統領は関与の必要性を理解している。彼は影響力が規則制定から生じること、そして、その未来および地域全体の未来を形づくるためには米国が機構に加わらなければならないことを認識している。

11 バイデン氏はまた、まずは新型コロナウイルス感染症（COVID−19）対策に取り組み、自国の競争力を立て直さなければならないことをわかっている。米国人は自由貿易とグローバリゼーションを尊重しているが、指導者らには中産階級と再びつながり、彼らの未来を安定させる助けになってほしいとも望んでいる。日本は、アジア地域とより深く統合するほど、国がもっと繁栄して安定することを米国がよりよく理解するための手助けをすべきである。それが戦後の日本の歩んできた道筋で、歴代の米政権によって奨励されてきたことだ。今度は同じ賢明な助言を（日本が）提供する番である。　　　　　　　　　　　　　　　　　　（訳・注　桑田）

次号予告『ジャパンタイムズ社説集 2021』

2021年度より、社説集は**年1回**の発行となります。
次号は掲載本数を増やして2021年12月に発売予定です。
詳細は決まり次第 BOOK CLUB でお知らせいたします。
https://bookclub.japantimes.co.jp/

ジャパンタイムズ社説集
―2020年下半期

2021年2月20日　初版発行

編　者　ジャパンタイムズ出版 英語出版編集部
　　　　© The Japan Times Publishing, Ltd., 2021
監　修　又江原 裕
発行者　伊藤 秀樹
発行所　株式会社 ジャパンタイムズ出版
　　　　〒102-0082 東京都千代田区一番町2-2 一番町第二 TG ビル 2F
　　　　電話　050-3646-9500（出版営業部）
　　　　ウェブサイト　https://jtpublishing.co.jp/
印刷所　日経印刷株式会社

本書の内容に関するお問い合わせは、上記ウェブサイトまたは郵便でお受けいたします。

定価はカバーに表示してあります。

万一、乱丁落丁のある場合は送料当社負担でお取り替えいたします。
（株）ジャパンタイムズ出版・出版営業部宛てにお送りください。

ISBN978-4-7890-1780-0
Printed in Japan

本書のご感想をお寄せください。
https://jtpublishing.co.jp/contact/comment/